NOTES AND COMMENTS
ON THE
DARDANELLES CAMPAIGN

WITH FOUR MAPS

BY

A. KEARSEY, D.S.O., O.B.E., *p.s.c.*

LATE LIEUTENANT-COLONEL, GENERAL STAFF

Four Shillings Nett
By Post 4/4

ALDERSHOT:
GALE & POLDEN, LTD., WELLINGTON WORKS
AND AT LONDON AND PORTSMOUTH

INTRODUCTION

The writer's qualifications for the task he has undertaken are mainly that for many years he has given great attention to all that has been written about the Gallipoli Campaign. He has also served in the Dardanelles, and has received much first-hand information to supplement personal experience.

The writer has endeavoured to follow the best authorities with impartiality and judgment. He is encouraged to make another addition to his historical works by the comment on his latest effort by " Fighting Forces," namely, that " the author has a well-deserved reputation for helping officers in their studies."

The writer would like to emphasize the point that the price of this little book prohibits an exhaustive treatise being made on the subject of this campaign. Nor is it possible to include elaborate maps.

These notes are only intended to be a guide to students, and it is hoped to interest them sufficiently to lead them to read the larger and important works by General Sir Ian Hamilton (" My Gallipoli Diary "), General Sir C. E. Callwell (" The Dardanelles "), General C. F. Aspinall-Oglander (" Official History of the Gallipoli Campaign "), Sir J. Arthur (" Life of Lord Kitchener "), and the " Dardanelles Commission Report."

Finally, gratitude must be expressed to the Publishers, Messrs. Gale & Polden, Ltd., for their co-operation and supervision, and for making it possible to issue these Notes to students at a very small cost.

For those who are making an extensive study of this Campaign the " Official History of the Gallipoli Campaign " cannot be too strongly recommended.

The frank expressions of opinion and the lucid form in which it is written make it not only an excellent story but an important addition to the literature of the war.

CONTENTS

PAGES

INTRODUCTION...   v

CHAPTER I.

THE ENTRY OF TURKEY INTO THE WAR ...   1-6

    Britain's difficulties in the Middle East.
    How Britain endeavoured to solve these difficulties.
    Difficulties of operations in the Gallipoli Peninsula.
    The general situation in 1915.
    The attitude of the Balkan States.
    The War Council's decision to start purely naval attacks.
    The general idea of the Dardanelles' campaign.
    The result of the fall of Constantinople.
    The value of a well-organized attack delivered by a combined naval and military force.
    Russia's appeal for help, and its influence on the War Council's decisions.
    The wish for Britain to operate independently with her naval power.
    Orders given to the Admiralty January 13th, 1915, to capture the Gallipoli Peninsula.

CHAPTER II.

NAVAL OPERATIONS   7-14

    Description of the Gallipoli Peninsula and Dardanelles.
    Description of our fleet.
    Movements of the *Gœben* and *Breslau*.
    British naval mission informed by the Turks that they were no longer required.
    Actions by the Turkish fleet in September and October.
    Naval operations on November 3rd and 18th.
    Destruction of Sedd el Bahr forts.
    Action of submarine B.11.
    Admiralty's decision by the end of 1914 to detach some of our largest ships to the Dardanelles.
    Lord Fisher's recommendations for an immediate attempt to force the Dardanelles with ships.
    January 13th, 1915: The plan for forcing the Dardanelles by the navy was approved by the War Council.
    Further decisions by the War Council on February 16th.

CONTENTS

PAGES

Naval operations on February 19th, 25th and 26th.
Landing by Royal Marines at Kum Kale and Sedd-el-Bahr.
Bombardment of intermediate defences up to Fort Dardanus on March 1st.
Destruction of guns at Kum Kale fort.
Naval operations March 4th to March 15th.
Final and biggest naval attack made on March 18th with available battleships.
The failure of this attack.
Decision to use the army available in the Eastern Mediterranean to co-operate in forcing the Straits.
Work of British submarines in the Straits.

CHAPTER III.

PLAN OF CAMPAIGN 15-19

Arrival of Sir Ian Hamilton at Tenedos, and conference with commanders of British fleet, French fleet and French troops.
The available forces of the Allies and Turks compared.
Strength of opposing forces compared.
Possible landing plans considered.
Requirements of artillery and ammunition necessary.
Difficulties with which the Commander-in-Chief would have to deal.
Reloading of ships at Alexandria and consequent delay.
Distribution of the Turks at the landing-places chosen for our troops.
The courses open to the Commander-in-Chief.
The reasons for carrying out the selected course.
The main drawbacks to landing at five different points at Helles.
The details of the plan for the landings.

CHAPTER IV.

THE LANDINGS 20-28

The Royal Naval Division arrived in the Gulf of Saros.
The Anzac Corps landed north of Gaba Tepe.
The operations of the Anzac Corps.
The difficulties of the Anzac troops on arrival at the summit of the cliffs overlooking their landing place.
The opposition by the 19th Turkish division.
The difficulties of holding the final position gained by the Anzac troops on a front of approximately two miles.
The decision by the Commander-in-Chief to maintain the position at Anzac.
The difficulties of operating in unknown country without artillery support.
Landing at Helles : description of " S," " V," " W," " X," " Y " Beaches.
Details of the landings at " S," " V," " W," " X ," " Y " Camber and Kum Kale Beaches.

CONTENTS ix

CHAPTER V.

PAGES

FIRST BATTLE OF KRITHIA 29-33

Capture of Hill 141.
Decision to withdraw French troops from Kum Kale.
Attempt by Anzac Troops to advance into "No-Man's" Land on 400 ft. Plateau.
Line on which Anzac troops were able to consolidate described.
The advance at Helles on April 27th.
Details of the new line gained at Helles from Eski Hissarlik to a point 500 yards south of Gully Ravine.
Dangers of a salient in a line.
Objectives described for the advance on April 28th.
Strength of the opposing Turks.
Summing-up of the situation after the first Battle of Krithia by Sir Ian Hamilton in his Despatches.
Causes of the failure of the first Battle of Krithia.
Dangers of starting operations with scanty information.
Dangers of starting operations without reserves at hand and without the possibility of surprising the enemy.
General Birdwood's suggestion for withdrawal from Anzac considered.
Difficulty of artillery support discussed.
Underestimation of Turkish resistance.

CHAPTER VI.

SECOND BATTLE OF KRITHIA 34-38

Consolidation of line continued.
Arrival of 29th India Brigade on May 1st.
Turk's attack at 2200 hours on May 1st.
Counter-attack by 29th Division at 0500 hours.
Turk's attacks on nights May 2/3 and May 3/4 repulsed.
Advance by 87th Brigade east of Gully Ravine.
Attempted advance by three battalions of the Anzac Corps on Hill 700 led to no gain of ground.
Fifty New Zealanders landed at Suvla Bay occupied Lala Baba.
Arrival at Helles of Lancashire Fusilier Brigade of the 42nd Territorial Division.
Second Battle of Krithia, May 6th, 7th, 8th, described.
Attack started 1100 hours, May 6th. In the centre our line was advanced four hundred yards and in other parts up to 300 yards.
Five Turkish divisions were at hand as reinforcements on May 7th.
Final efforts to capture Krithia failed.
Positions gained were consolidated.
Heavy casualties owing to enemy's machine guns and our limited land artillery support.

CONTENTS

PAGES

Difficulty of two offensives, namely, on the Western Front and at Gallipoli.
Strength of the Turks positions, their armament and numbers were realized.
Bad weather would affect landing of our ammunition.
Sir Ian Hamilton's report on necessity of consolidation and fortification of our front.
Attacks made by Anzac troops between May 6th and 11th.
Sufficient men now not available for the capture of either Achi Baba or Chunuk Bair.
Reorganization of areas, their communications and landing-places now carried out.

CHAPTER VII.

OPERATIONS UP TO END OF JUNE 39-46

Division of Helles front into four sectors.
Beginning of trench warfare.
Capture of strong Turkish redoubt north-east of Beach "Y" on May 12th.
Lord Kitchener's report to War Council that available troops spared from England required in France.
Considerations by War Council as to whether Gallipoli Campaign should be abandoned, or not.
Review of the situation by the Commander-in-Chief.
Arrival of German "U" Boats with bases in the Adriatic.
British battleships sunk during May.
Less support now for Allied troops from naval guns.
Reinforcements and stores had to be brought from Mudros in small craft to various landing-places.
Difficulties of the campaign were increased.
Russian army assembled at Odessa for operations near Constantinople was sent to Galicia.
52nd Division sent out from England to Gallipoli.
Attack by Turks on night May 18/19th on the Anzac front.
Anzac forward positions now adequately secured.
Armistice arranged for a day with the Turks for the burial of their dead.
Realization that large reinforcements of men, munitions and war material would be required if Allies were to achieve their object in Gallipoli.
Difficulty of supplying wants in a secondary area of operations.
Summing-up of the situation by the Commander-in-Chief as to the tactical basis of future plans.
The increasing strength of the enemy was now recognized so that three divisions of the new armies and the infantry of two Territorial divisions were to be sent out as reinforcements to the Dardanelles.
Preparations for June 4th offensive.
Battle of June 4th described.

CONTENTS   xi

PAGES

Superiority of enemy's artillery and increasing strength of resistance prevented any great gain of ground which was limited to an advance of approximately four hundred yards in the centre.
Turkish counter-attacks during following ten days were directed to regain lost ground.
Night June 11/12th two lines of trenches were won on front of 29th Division.
Capture of Haricot Redoubt by 2nd Division of the French Corps while 1st Division captured six hundred yards of Turkish trenches above Kereves Dere.
Effective demonstration carried out on the afternoon of June 28th.
At Helles five lines of Turkish trenches, about two hundred prisoners, three mountain guns were captured on June 28th.
Turkish counter-attacks on the two following nights were unsuccessful.
Determined Turkish attack on night June 29/30th at Anzac and throughout June 30th.
Turks incurred heavy losses.
The result was that the next month was quiet on the Anzac front.
At Helles the French Corps advanced their line and captured the Quadrilateral east of the source of the Keerves Dere.

CHAPTER VIII.

JULY PLANS AND PREPARATIONS 47-51

General review of the situation at end of June.
Turkish positions were being made more formidable up to the Bulair from those opposing our troops in Keerves and Saghir ravines.
Casualties were increasing owing to heat, dust and flies.
Divisions were below strength, no adequate provision of fresh drafts, lack of artillery support.
When reinforcements arrived the Allied army would include thirteen divisions, four Anzac mounted brigades, and one Indian brigade.
Distribution of troops to be assigned to Helles, Anzac and Suvla.
Turks had nine divisions under his command.
War Council decide to continue offensive operations in Gallipoli.
Fresh plan considered for utilizing the services of the reinforcements.
General plan was first to capture Sari Bair and then to gain a position astride the Peninsula from Gaba Tepe to the straits north of Maidos.
Turks attacked at Helles on July 5th and suffered great loss.

CONTENTS

PAGES

July 12th and 13th: operations similar to those undertaken on June 28th were carried out.
British lost three thousand casualties and advanced two to four hundred yards on different parts of the front.
Considerations for the possible courses to be followed by the Commander-in-Chief discussed.
When expected reinforcements arrive a hundred and seven thousand rifles and a hundred and ninety four guns would be available.
Decision reached was to reinforce the Anzac Corps and to take the offensive with troops landing in Suvla to capture the dominating heights of Sari Bair.
Discussion as to the possible courses and the reason for adopting the plan of landing at Suvla Bay.
The tactical scheme was sound and was the best of the four considered.
Contributory reasons for failure discussed.
Available troops at Helles, Anzac and Suvla detailed.
Landing arrangements for troops made during July.
Devices practised to mislead enemy as to the main intentions of the operations.
Naval demonstrations at Mitylene.
Surprise landing at Gulf of Saros.

CHAPTER IX.

OFFENSIVE OPERATIONS AT ANZAC AND HELLES ... 52-58

Operations at Helles starting at 1600 hours, August 6th.
Commander-in-Chief moved his headquarters to Imbros.
Reasons for this move.
Important factor for success was the rapidity with which the Allies could gain objectives.
Dispersion of Turks and organization of the forces under Liman von Sander's command.
Main attack at Helles repulsed and small gains on the left flank had to be relinquished when Turks counter-attacked.
General plan for the operations at Anzac for the attack against Turks' positions on Sari Bair and from 400 Plateau to Nek.
Landing of 10th Division (less one brigade) and 11th Division at Suvla Bay night August 6/7th.
Description from Despatches of operations against Turks' trenches on the 400 Plateau.
Assaults by 2nd Australian Brigade and a Light Horse regiment contained Turkish reserves although no ground was gained.
Details of the operations of the four columns on the night August 6/7th advancing towards the summit of Sari Bair from the northern end of Anzac on the shore near No. 2 Outpost.
Description in Despatches by Commander-in-Chief of the preliminary operations.

CONTENTS   xiii

PAGES

Surprise and capture at the outset of operations of Turkish posts on the lower spurs.
Difficulties of reaching the objectives on Chunuk Bair and Hill 305.
Capture of Turkish Post No. 3 by Auckland Mounted Rifles.
Capture of Bauchop's Hill and Table Top by the New Zealand Mounted Rifle Brigade.
Capture of Damakjelik Bair by South Wales Borderers.
Capture of Rhododendron Spur by 0530 hours, August 7th.
Capture by 4th Australian Brigade of northern end of Azmak Dere and by 29th Indian Infantry of lower slopes of Hill " Q " by 0700 hours, August 7th.
Enemy on summit of main ridge of Chunuk Bair not surprised.
Rearrangement of Anzac forces into right, centre and left columns.
Operations of the three columns.
No. 1 Column unable to retain position won on the crest of Chunuk Bair.
Relief of No. 1 Column.
Relieving troops heavily shelled on August 10th before they had settled down, and then attacked by 8th Turkish Division and three additional battalions.
Turks regained positions on Chunuk Bair.
Report by the *Commander-in-Chief as to failure of the offensive for the capture of Sari Bair and the advance to the Narrows.*
Junction effected with troops landed at Suvla on August 12th.

CHAPTER X.

OPERATIONS AT SUVLA BAY   59-66

Landing at Suvla Bay started at 2230 hours on August 6th.
Strength of Turks estimated at 4,000 on Hill 10, on ridge beyond Suvla Point, round Lala Baba on a knoll between Salt Lake and Nibrunesi Point, on Chocolate Hill and Ismail Oglu Tepe.
General Plan for the landing at " A," " B " and " C " Beaches before dawn on August 7th.
Objectives for 11th Division described.
Objectives for remainder of IX Corps described.
Landings by 32nd and 33rd Brigades at " C " Beach.
Landing by 34th Brigade at " A " Beach.
Capture of Lala Baba.
Attack against Turkish positions on Hill 10 eventually captured by two battalions of the 34th Brigade.
Advance on to the Karakol Dagh.
Retreat of Turks towards Sulajik and Kuchuk Anafarta Ova.

CONTENTS

PAGES

Landing of the 31st Brigade and two battalions of the 30th Brigade near Nibrunesi Point after dawn on August 7th.
Advance of 31st Brigade to support left flank of 34th Brigade.
Disembarkation of remainder of 10th Division after 0800 hours near " A " Beach and near Ghazi Baba.
Operations of 10th Division for the capture of Chocolate and Green Hills and for the 34th and 32nd Divisions against Kuchuk Anafarta.
Capture of Chocolate Hill.
Increasing Turkish opposition at Ismail Oglu Tepe.
Difficulties of the operations for the 11th Division discussed.
Description of situation on August 8th from Despatches.
Occupation of Scimitar Hill by two battalions of 32nd Brigade.
10th Division advanced their positions on Kiretch Tepe Sirt.
Reasons given for not advancing on August 8th.
Artillery support discussed with a reference on this subject from Despatches.
Arrival at Suvla on evening of August 8th by the Commander-in-Chief.
Result of aeroplane reconnaissance was that Turks were removing guns back to other positions and that reinforcements were coming up from Bulair.
Opportunity missed on August 8th by IX Corps to capture heights east of their landing places.
Commander-in-Chief on arrival at Suvla urged that an immediate attack on the Turks' positions on the Anafarta Hills.
Concentration of the 32nd Brigade for an attack on Anafarta Hills caused their battalions to be withdrawn from advantageous positions on Hill 70 and on Abrikja Spur.
32nd Brigade attack started 0400 hours on August 9th.
Tekke Tepe, commanding the Anafarta Sagir, was captured.
31st Brigade gained a footing on Scimitar Hill, but could not maintain their position there.
Position gained by 33rd Brigade on Ismail Oglu Tepe soon after 0500 hours on August 9th.
Attacks by Turkish 12th Division.
Recapture by Turks of Ismail Oglu Tepe and Scimitar Hill.
Withdrawal of 32nd Brigade to Sulajik.
Withdrawal of 33rd Brigade and two battalions 34th Brigade to Chocolate Hill.
Result of fighting on August 9th was that 11th Division was back in its original position after having suffered heavy losses.
Attack on August 10th by 53rd Division supported by 11th Division and 59th Field Brigade R.A., two mountain batteries and naval guns.

CONTENTS xv

PAGES

Ground was gained at the outset by the 53rd Division and had to be relinquished later.
Consolidation of line from the Azmak Dere through Green Hill and west of Kuchuk Anafarta Ova to the position held by the 10th Division on the Kiretch Tepe Sirt.
54th Division ordered to make a night march and dawn attack on August 13th on Turkish positions at Kavak Tepe and Tekke Tepe.
163rd Brigade first cleared the ground north of Sulajik.
Enemy opposition was so strong in this area that the night march and attack were abandoned.
Reasons for giving up the night operation by the 54th Division.
Attack by 30th and 31st Brigades along the top of the Kiretch Tepe Sirt ridge supported on the right by 162nd Brigade enabled the 10th Division to gain ground on the left flank.
Value of hand grenades was brought to notice in the fighting in intersected country.
Troops in Suvla area settled down to trench warfare. Further reinforcements were refused and so the fate of the Dardanelles enterprise was practically settled.
Final line held by the IX Corps in the Suvla Bay area ran from Azmak Dere, through Hetman Chair, Green Hill, Sulajik and Kuchuk Anafarta Ova over Kiretch Tepe Sirt to the sea.

CHAPTER XI.

OPERATIONS AND PLANS LEADING TO THE EVACUATION 67-72

Indecision as to future operations after the deadlock at Suvla.
Commander-in-Chief asked for 45,000 men to replace casualties and a further 50,000 in addition.
Three alternative rôles were considered for the troops in Gallipoli.
29th Division were moved by night from Helles to Suvla.
2nd Mounted Division were brought from Egypt to Suvla.
Five divisions now under the command of the General de Lisle at Suvla Bay.
On August 21st, 53rd and 54th Divisions were to contain the enemy on their front between Sulajik

and Kiretch Tepe Sirt. The 29th and 11th Divisions were to advance respectively from Chocolate Hill and from Azmak Dere. 10th and 2nd Mounted Divisions were in Corps reserve.

The Anzac Corps were to advance on the left of their line from Damakjelik Bair to the line Kabak Kuyu and Susak Kuyu.

The attack on August 21st described.

Turks were not surprised by our attack. They were supported by forty-eight guns and eight 5-inch howitzers. They had observation over all the ground over which our troops advanced.

On the Anzac side a force consisting of the 29th Indian Infantry Brigade, New Zealand Mounted Rifles and units from the 10th and 13th Divisions, advanced towards Hill 60 beyond Damakjelik Bair.

The positions gained made it possible during the next few days to join the left of the Anzac front to the right of the Suvla front on the northern side of Azmak Dere.

Anzac Corps was strengthened by arrival of the 2nd Australian Division composed of two infantry brigades.

August 27th: a continuous line of trenches for twelve miles was linked up from close to Gaba Tepe to the Gulf of Saros at the foot of Kiretch Tepe Sirt.

Drawbacks of the present position.

August offensive had been at a cost of 40,000 men. Allies' losses were not replaced.

Reasons for the lack of success.

Superiority of the Turks in rifles and in artillery.

Available artillery of the Allies would not be sufficient to render them temporarily untenable.

Communication would become more difficult as the autumn advanced.

Health of the troops was suffering.

Existing formations were 30,000 below strength.

September 25th: the Commander-in-Chief was informed that two British divisions and probably one French division must be sent to Salonika—another theatre of operations.

October 11th: the Commander-in-Chief was asked for his views as to the evacuation of the Peninsula.

Rival claims of Gallipoli and Salonika considered as a subsidiary theatre of operations.

October 16th: General Sir Ian Hamilton received orders to return to England.

October 28th: General Sir Charles Monro arrived at Imbros to command the forces.

Situation at Salonika.

Severe storm started on November 27th, followed by rain and then by a north wind and snow blizzard for three days.

In the following week 10,000 sick were evacuated.

General Monro gave an opinion as to the advisability of evacuating the Peninsula before the winter set in

CONTENTS xvii

PAGES

CHAPTER XII

THE EVACUATION 73-79
    The difficulties of embarking three army corps discussed.
    Quotation from General Monro's despatches as to the dangers of the positions occupied by our troops.
    Naval authorities unwilling to agree to the evacuation of Helles added to the difficulties of the War Council.
    Lord Kitchener's visit to Gallipoli.
    His endorsement of General Monro's opinion.
    Arrangements to be made for evacuation of Anzac and Suvla by the night of December 19/20th.
    Defensive positions constructed at Suvla and Anzac.
    Arrangements for holding front line trenches during the final phase of the operations.
    Orders received on December 28th to evacuate Helles area.
    Turkish and Allies forces compared.
    Relief of the French infantry.
    Gradual reduction of the fighting forces at Helles up to the night of January 8/9th.
    Turks become accustomed to a certain nightly routine of artillery, machine gun and rifle fire combined with bombing.
    Instructions as to actual evacuation quoted from naval despatches dated January 26th, 1916.
    Arrangements for intermediate posts on the lines of withdrawal to " V," " W " and Gully Beaches.
    Work of the Royal Engineers in keeping the pier facilities intact to enable the navy to carry out their rôle in the general plan.
    Arrangements for withdrawal to " V," " W " and Gully Beaches.
    Establishment of posts between de Totts' Battery and Gully Beach.
    Attack on January 7th by the 12th Turkish Division against our 13th Division gave the enemy no information as to our intention to evacuate our positions at Helles.
    Final arrangements for embarkation at 2000 hours, at 2130 hours and at 0300 hours.
    Casualties incurred on the Peninsula.
    Report by the Prime Minister in the House of Commons on January 10th, 1916.
    General Monro's special order after the evacuation.

CHAPTER XIII.

DETAILED LIST OF TROOPS ENGAGED IN THE GALLIPOLI CAMPAIGN... 80-88

xviii   CONTENTS

                                                    PAGES
                    CHAPTER XIV.
LIST OF DATES   89-105
      September 4th, 1914, to June 6th, 1915.

                    CHAPTER XV.
LIST OF DATES   106-124
      June 7th, 1915, to end of Campaign.

                    CHAPTER XVI.
COMMENTS   125-141
      On the general situation at the end of 1914.
      On the origin of the campaign.
      On the situation in January, 1915.
      On the Cabinet decision of the 13th January, 1915.
      On the situation in February, 1915.
      On the Cabinet decision of 16th February, 1915.
      On the naval operations.
      On the Commander-in-Chief's plan for the landings
          at Helles and Anzac.
      On the Landings, 25th April 1915.
      On the War Council's decision in May and June, 1915.
      On the considerations governing the employment of
          reinforcements in a new offensive.
      On the plan of operations for an August offensive.
      On the attack at Helles.
      On the Anzac operations.
      On the Suvla operations.
      On the events leading to the evacuation.
      On the evacuation of Anzac and Suvla.
      On the evacuation of Helles.
      On the lessons of the campaign.

                    LIST OF MAPS

ANZAC   ...   .   ⎫ AT
THE LANDINGS. Situation at dusk 25th April   ⎬ END
HELLES. The Beaches and the Turkish Defences, ⎪ OF
    25th December, 1915   ...   .   ⎪ BOOK
SUVLA. 8 a.m., 7th AUGUST   ...   .   ⎭

CHAPTER I.

THE ENTRY OF TURKEY INTO THE WAR.

When Turkey entered the war at the end of October, 1914, as Germany's ally, Britain's difficulties in the Middle East were enormously increased.

The questions of policy which then became urgent, were the defence of the naval position in the eastern Mediterranean, the security of the Suez Canal and Persian Gulf from Turkish attacks, and the necessity of retaining the loyalty of the Mohammedan world population over half of which Britain ruled, and of which the Sultan of Turkey was the chief.

In addition, the most direct means of communication between Russia and her Allies was cut off.

For many months in the year it was not possible to get into touch with the Russians either through the ice-bound port of Archangel, or by the small ports on the Murman coast or through Siberia.

Britain endeavoured to solve these problems by a campaign in the Gallipoli Peninsula, by an advance up the River Tigris from Fao towards Mosul, and from the Suez Canal towards Aleppo.

It was hoped that the appearance of an Allied Fleet at Constantinople would disorganize the Ottoman Government and cause its flight to Asia Minor, and that the Balkan States would then join the Allies in operations against Turkey.

This hope was strengthened by the tentative offer from Venizelos, then Prime Minister of Greece, to supply a Greek division for these operations.

It was not realized at the time of the inception of the idea of a campaign against Turkey that there was an army of approximately 200,000 men in the vicinity of Constantinople after the Turks began to mobilize; and that when our attacks on the Dardanelles started the Turkish Army was not heavily engaged elsewhere.

During 1914, 800,000 men were called up for service.

No large forces had been sent either to Transcaucasia, to Egypt or to Mesopotamia.

Therefore, they had available the bulk of their army for operations wherever they were attacked in the vicinity of their capital.

The country of the Gallipoli Peninsula was most unsuitable

for military operations. Water was scarce, good roads were non-existent, and the hills were overgrown with brushwood.

There was little scope for extended movements or for troops to make use of their mobility, so, consequently, the defenders had every advantage of ground in the manner in which the military operations were undertaken.

The ravines and valleys for the most part are at right angles to the line of advance of troops from Helles to the Bulair lines.

Thus the distance of fifty-two miles in a line between these two points was multiplied owing to the necessity for troops having to descend in many cases to sea level, when they have reached the top of one hill before climbing the next one.

These hills gradually rose from our landing points round Cape Helles to Achi Baba, 709 feet, up to Sari Bair, 971 feet, dominating Anzac Cove up to Uveik Dagh, 1,141 feet, eight miles further north-east.

On arrival at the Bulair lines our troops would be faced with a formidable obstacle only three miles wide, strongly entrenched and with both flanks resting on the sea.

As there were no parallels for amphibious warfare in a barren country the difficulties were under-estimated.

Another point for consideration is whether this offensive campaign should have been undertaken in view of our commitments on the Western Front and of the necessity of adhering to the principle of economy of force in strategy as well as in tactics.

Our main enemy must always have been Germany, whose defeat alone would have ended the war.

Therefore, it is permissible to conclude that all efforts should have been made only on that front.

The situation, however, as has already been noted, had become complicated by the entry of Turkey into the war. It was necessary then to operate in other parts of the Empire and to check Turkish and German ambitions on sea and land. The point then would be how far should these operations go in order to fulfil our necessary obligations and to carry out sound strategy.

In 1915 we had not sufficient superiority of strength to hope to break through the strong German line between the North Sea and the Alps.

It might be possible to gain an early decision against the Turks, and by so doing open up communications with the Russians and cause hesitating neutrals in the Balkan States to join us. The Balkan countries were still postponing their choice of friends.

THE DARDANELLES CAMPAIGN 3

The position of Serbia was precarious if Bulgaria mobilized her army of 300,000 and joined the Allies.

Roumania's position was of great strategic importance, as through it lay the direct route between Berlin and Constantinople to Baghdad and the Persian Gulf.

Also Roumania had an army of 350,000 and had large resources of grain and oil.

The Greeks had an army of 180,000 and was waiting to see what the probable result of the war was likely to be.

The Bulgarians in the past had suffered from the Turks and Roumanians, and so they too were waiting for the situation to develop.

The attitude of the Balkan States might definitely have been turned in our favour if this amphibious campaign had started when war with Turkey was declared, instead of on April 25th, 1915.

In defence of the War Council's decision to start purely naval attacks on November 3rd, 1914, it must be noted that Lord Kitchener favoured the idea and reported that no troops were then available for this campaign; and that Lord Fisher did not officially offer any objection to the proposal or record his opinion at the initial Council Meeting that the enterprise was not likely to succeed.

In support of Lord Kitchener's views it is now clear that an immediate attack in force by sea and land towards the Turkish capital might have brought great results, which could not possibly have been obtained elsewhere.

Had the attack by the Navy and Army been simultaneous in favourable weather, an overwhelming success might have been achieved.

Therefore, the general idea of the Dardanelles campaign was sound, and did not violate the principle of economy of force by unnecessarily dissipating our resources in an enterprise which did not subserve the main operation. In this connection the First Lord of the Admiralty, Mr. Churchill, said in a speech at Dundee, with reference to the Dardanelles campaign: " You must not forget the prize, for which you are contending. The Army and the fleet are separated only by a few miles from a victory such as this war has not yet seen. I am speaking of victory in the sense of a brilliant and formidable fact, shaping the destinies of nations, and shortening the duration of the war. Beyond those few miles of ridge and scrub lie the downfall of a hostile Empire, the destruction of an enemy's fleet and army, the fall of a world-famous capital, and probably the accession of powerful allies. There was never a great subsidiary operation of war in which a more complete harmony of strategic, political, and economic advantages has combined, or which stood in truer relation to the main decision, which is in the central theatre. Through the Narrows of the Dardanelles and across the ridges of the Gallipoli Peninsula lie some of the shortest paths to a triumphant peace."

This was a correct statement as to the theory on which the Dardanelles operations were based. It is not concerned with the methods adopted to carry out the objective and the strength and distribution of the forces engaged, or whether the problem of the supply of men and ammunition was carefully thought out when the operations were planned, or whether the War Council was justified in arriving at the decision to order an attack of naval forces alone.

It cannot be gainsaid that the fall of Constantinople and the destruction of the Turks' power in Europe would have had a vital effect on the war.

The political and strategical motives for the operations were adequate.

There were undoubtedly great results to be obtained, but the practicability of the means by which the desired end was sought required detailed consideration before the decision was reached.

A successful attack would probably have caused the hesitating neutrals in the Balkans to join the Allies.

In 1914 and early in 1915 the Turks had given little attention to their defences.

Therefore, a well-organized attack delivered in sufficient strength by a combined naval and military force at the time when the first naval bombardments took place might have changed the whole fortunes of the war in our favour, and would have led directly to the defeat of Germany.

As it was the two months' warning given by the fleet after the naval attack in February, 1915, enabled the Turks and Germans to make our task on April 25th extremely difficult. Also, it must be noted that the margin between success and failure was small on April 25th.

On April 26th the Turks could not have resisted vigorous attacks at Helles, and on May 5th they nearly vacated Krithia and Achi Baba.

An important point to be noted with reference to the decision for undertaking this Campaign is that on January 2nd, 1915, Russia asked for help; and this request was the predominating cause of the attack on the Dardanelles.

THE DARDANELLES CAMPAIGN 5

The statement by the British Ambassador in Russia has an important bearing on the decision to undertake the Dardanelles expedition. It was as follows:—

" When Turkey declared war Russia turned to Great Britain with a request that she would divert a portion of the Turkish troops from the Caucasus by means of a counter-demonstration at some other point. The operations at the Dardanelles were undertaken with a double object—on the one hand of reducing the pressure of the Turks in the Caucasus, and, on the other, of opening the Straits and so making it possible for Russia to export her grain and receive foreign products, of which she stands in need."

It must be noted that although the Turkish offensive in the Caucasus was checked by the end of December, 1914, and was not renewed until after the summer of 1915, it was due to the Allies' attacks on the Dardanelles.

Our operations helped the morale of the Russian nation at a time when their armies in Galicia and Poland were being driven back.

Although the desire to help Russia was a predominating cause of the attack on the Dardanelles, yet these were contributory influences.

On the Western Front the British Expeditionary Force was not able to make any progress on its thirty miles of front. Owing to the static warfare between the North Sea and the Alps neither side could move without heavy loss and great expenditure of resources.

It was, therefore, considered that with the help of some of the British ships, which could not compete in a modern naval battle in the North Sea owing to lack of speed and armament, a diversion might be attempted elsewhere.

There were 70,000 men in Egypt. The Turkish attacks on the Suez Canal on February 3rd and 4th, 1915, had been easily repulsed by less than half these troops.

Therefore, it was suggested that as the bulk of these large forces would now be inactive, and as the Gallipoli Peninsula was accessible to Egypt, operations there would safeguard the Suez Canal by drawing off the Turkish armies operating in Egypt and Palestine.

In addition, Britain would be operating in an independent expedition, in which her naval power would give the valuable support required for an early success.

The commander of the German fleet has recorded his opinion that the forcing of the Dardanelles would have led to decisive results.

At any rate our ships outside Constantinople could have destroyed the Zeitun Burner S.A.A. and shell factory, the Pera Galata gun and S.A. factory, and the powder mills at Makir Keni.

If Turkey's sole source of ammunition supply had been cut off her military position would have been untenable. The defeat of Turkey would have been a step towards the downfall of Germany. It might, then, have been possible to turn Germany's flank via Austria-Hungary through the Dardenelles and Constantinople with the help of Greece, Roumania, Bulgaria, Italy, Serbia and Russia.

Accordingly, on January 13th, 1915, the plan for forcing the Dardanelles was approved by the War Council. Orders were given to the Admiralty " to bombard and take the Gallipoli Peninsula with Constantinople as its objective."

Thus, unfortunately, the conditions as to concentration of naval and military force were not fulfilled.

CHAPTER II.

NAVAL OPERATIONS.

THE Gallipoli Peninsula runs in a south-westerly direction. From Cape Tekke, at the toe of the Peninsula, to the Bulair lines the distance is fifty-two miles.

Its greatest width is twelve miles, and it tapers down to three miles at Bulair.

The coast from Cape Helles to Suvla, with which our landing operations are concerned, is rocky. The cliffs range from one hundred to three hundred feet in height. On the eastern side of the Peninsula the cliffs are less pronounced, and the ground slopes less steeply to the sea.

Where our operations took place there were few sandy beaches. These are on either side of Gaba Tepe and at Suvla Bay; three are within two miles and north of Cape Tekke and two are between Cape Tekke and Sedd-el-Bahr, and one is at Eski Hissarlik, on the eastern side of Morto Bay.

The factors more nearly affecting the naval problems are the Dardanelles, including the Narrows and the Straits of Gallipoli.

The Dardanelles are forty-one miles long, with an average breadth of two miles.

The width of the Narrows is sixteen hundred yards between the two forts Chanak and Kilid Bahr.

The maximum width is in Eren Keui Bay, four miles from the toe of the Peninsula.

The naval authorities had arranged to carry out three definite operations. First, the batteries at the southern end of the Dardanelles at Cape Helles and Sedd-el-Bahr on the Peninsula and Kum Kale, Orkanie Mound, and Yeni Shehr on the Asiatic side were to be silenced.

Then the minefields higher up the Dardanelles were to be swept, and the land batteries were to be destroyed.

Finally, the forts and mines in the Narrows were to be dealt with.

Our fleet finally included a French squadron of battleships, a Russian cruiser, the *Queen Elizabeth*, with eight 15-inch guns, the *Inflexible*, with eight 12-inch guns, the *Agamemnon* and *Lord Nelson*, each with ten 9.2-inch guns; a proportion of cruisers, a flotilla of destroyers, some minesweepers, and other small vessels.

Our ships mounted in all 274 guns.

On August 6th the Turkish ships *Goeben* and *Breslau* left Messina, and evaded the British ships which sighted them.

On August 10th the *Goeben* and *Breslau* arrived in the Dardanelles.

Britain demanded that these ships should be interned or forced to leave the Straits.

The Turks replied that they had bought these ships, but that they would send back the German crews to Berlin.

On August 15th the British Naval Mission was informed by the Turkish Government that it would no longer be required for executive command.

The Turkish Fleet now became under German control.

On August 22nd a British squadron was ordered to watch the Dardanelles.

The British Government decided that so long as German crews remained in the *Goeben* and *Breslau* no Turkish warship would be allowed to leave the Dardanelles.

On September 27th the gaps in two more minefields were filled up, and a fourth line was added to the existing ones.

Contrary to treaty agreements, the Turkish Government decreed that no vessels were to be permitted to enter the Straits.

On October 27th the Turkish fleet entered the Black Sea.

On October 29th attacks were made by the Turkish fleet against Odessa and Sevastopol. A Russian minelayer and a gunboat were sunk.

On October 30th, British, French and Russian Ambassadors demanded their passports. It is suggested that at this time it would have been possible to open up communication with our ally, the Russians, through the Dardanelles.

The importance of the Dardanelles in the World War was not yet fully appreciated.

On November 3rd there was a bombardment at a range of six miles by the French and British squadrons of the forts at the entrance to the Dardanelles.

The Sedd-el-Bahr forts were destroyed.

The effect of this bombardment on the Turkish Government was unfortunate, as it focussed their attention on the necessity of strengthening the naturally strong positions overlooking the Narrows; as there was little doubt now as to the menace to the capital through the Dardanelles.

On November 18th there was a naval battle, in which the *Goeben was damaged.*

On December 13th one of our submarines, B.11, entered the Straits of Gallopoli, and passing under five rows of Turkish mines torpedoed a Turkish warship.

THE DARDANELLES CAMPAIGN 9

German and Turkish officers had now elaborated schemes of defence, and had started to convert the positions in the Peninsula and in Turkey-in-Asia into strong fortresses owing to the warning which these naval operations had given of the possible major military operations either on Gallipoli or in Asia Minor.

By the end of 1914 a decision was reached by the Admiralty that it would be safe to detach some of our largest ships for operations in the Dardanelles. Unfortunately, no decision was made to carry through the proposal to advance on Constantinople, via Gallipoli, with a military force, supported by a fleet, until two months later. By that time the Turks were prepared. The Government had, however, received an assurance that the Western Front was secure. It was suggested that Germany might be struck through Turkey. The arguments were started, on the one hand, that the deadlock on the Western Front might be met by carrying out a subsidiary operation from the Mediterranean, either based on Salonika or on a port in Dalmatia, or on the Syrian coast; on the other hand, that the Western Front was the decisive theatre of war, to which all available personnel and munitions should be sent to support our Allies, the French, in holding the trench line, to secure the Channel ports, and to take the first opportunity of breaking through the German lines when we had sufficient reserves of men and ammunition for the purpose. These points were thought out for many weeks while the naval operations continued, and the Turkish forts daily were being strengthened.

On January 2nd, 1915, a telegram was received from Russia asking for a demonstration to be made against the Turks in order to ease the situation in the Caucasus.

Lord Kitchener's reply to this telegram was that a demonstration would be made.

This emphasized the point of making the Dardanelles the scene of our operations, as it was the only place in which it would be possible to stop reinforcements going in an easterly direction from Turkey.

Lord Fisher recommended an immediate attempt to force the Dardanelles with ships, and an army of 75,000 men from the Western Front, with the Greek troops, should land on the Peninsula and, with the Bulgarians, march on Adrianople, while the Roumanians and Serbs helped the Russians in their attacks on Austria.

The situation, however, could not be so easily settled, as the 75,000 men from France were not available, nor were the Greeks, Bulgarians and Roumanians ready for war, or definitely certain on which side to enter when they were fully mobilized.

On January 13th the plan for forcing the Dardanelles by the navy was approved by the War Council.

By the end of January we had seized the Turkish island of Tenedos and occupied the Greek island of Lemnos, respectively twenty miles south of and fifty miles south-west of Cape Helles. These islands were valuable as advanced bases.

On February 16th it was decided by the War Council to concentrate troops in the vicinity of the Dardanelles to be used as occasion might require. The 29th Division were to be sent to Mudros. Lord Kitchener, however, would not sanction their departure until March 10th. It would seem that there was still doubt in his mind as to the wisdom of concentrating our available reserves for this campaign.

On February 19th a bombardment was made by five British and three French battleships against the outer forts at the entrance to the Dardanelles.

The gunfire of the ships was observed by the seaplanes using the *Royal Ark* as an aircraft carrier.

The results of this bombardment were not conclusive. The Turks did not reply to the long-range fire, and when the ships steamed nearer to the shore for a closer bombardment their guns started to shoot, and it was then obvious that no serious damage had been inflicted on the enemy's fortifications. The Turks evacuated the outer forts.

On the morning of February 25th three battleships renewed the bombardment on the Turkish forts at Cape Helles, at Sedd-el-Bahr, and against Kum Kale and Fort Orkanie. These fortresses were now well provided with concealed heavy guns.

At Kum Kale there were four 10.2-inch guns and two 5.9-inch guns. At Fort Orkanie there were two 9.2-inch guns. At Cape Helles there were two 9.2-inch guns. At Chanak there were altogether in the two forts four 14-inch and nine 4-inch guns, one 8.2-inch gun, and four 5.9-inch guns. At Sedd-el-Bahr there were six 10.2-inch guns and two 5.9-inch guns. At Cape Helles there were two 9.2-inch guns. In the intervening ground between these two forts a field battery had been posted.

Our ships were able to bring into action fifteen and twelve-inch guns. The *Queen Elizabeth* could fire at ranges from which the land guns could not touch them.

Later in the day of February 25th six more ships reinforced

THE DARDANELLES CAMPAIGN

the original attackers, and steamed into close range of the forts, whose guns were silenced by 1700 hours, four of them being put out of action.

On the following day three ships continued the bombardment from inside the Straits, and steamed up to the entrance of the Narrows towards Dardanus, five miles south-west of Chanak. This fort, containing four 5.9-inch guns, was shelled.

Landing parties of the Royal Marines landed at Kum Kale, and destroyed one field gun and two anti-aircraft guns. At the same time a party of seventy-five Marines landed at Sedd-el-Bahr, and destroyed four heavy and two field guns near Tekke Burnu.

The results of this day's operations were more satisfactory than on previous days in that the entrance to the Straits had been cleared. The enemy's main defences, however, covering the Narrows at Chanak, Dardanus, Kephez Point and Fort Soghandere, were untouched.

These defences dominating the narrow channel were strong and well concealed. They could be supported by torpedoes and mines drifting with the prevalent wind in a south-westerly direction towards any ships attempting to steam up the Dardanelles.

In such a narrow defile the ships could not manœuvre freely, and would consequently be an easy mark for the Turkish guns in the fortresses commanding the Narrows.

On March 1st four battleships again entered the Straits and bombarded the intermediate defences up to Fort Dardanus. The results, however, were not satisfactory owing to the harassing fire from concealed land batteries.

A demolition party was landed at Kum Kale, with an escort of Marines. This party was able to destroy seven guns at Kum Kale Fort; also an abandoned field battery, four Nordenfeldts and a searchlight.

On the same day four French battleships bombarded the Bulair lines from the Gulf of Saros.

On the following day the bombardment was continued, and the Turkish barracks on the eastern side of the lines were destroyed by fire.

On March 3rd a landing party at Sedd-el-Bahr destroyed a fifteen-pounder battery.

It was now estimated that forty Turkish guns had been destroyed.

The main naval effort was made on March 18th.

In the meantime, naval operations were carried out on March 4th, 5th, 6th, 7th, 10th, 11th and 15th.

On the first of these dates the Forts Dardanus and Soghandere were bombarded by British ships, while the French cruiser bombarded Gaba Tepe. Besika, in Besika Bay, was also shelled in order to induce a relief in the minds of the Turkish Commander-in-Chief that this was a possible landing place.

Detachments of the Plymouth Battalion landed at Kum Kale and Sedd-el-Bahr were unable, owing to Turkish opposition, to do any further damage to these forts.

On the following day a demonstration was made by bombarding the outer forts of Smyrna in order to cause the Turks to maintain troops in this area.

Some ships also steamed up towards Kilid Bahr, where they came under fire from this fortress.

On March 6th five ships bombarded Dardanus and Soghandere Forts, while a simultaneous bombardment with aeroplane observation was carried out from the western side of the Gallipoli Peninsula by three ships, including the *Queen Elizabeth*, carrying eight 15-inch guns, against the Chanak and Kilid Bahr Forts from the Gulf of Saros.

The results were not substantial. The Turks replied to our fire with some effect from their land howitzers on the Peninsula, and were able to register direct hits on our ships. Seaplanes co-operated throughout the day, with the *Queen Elizabeth* firing at a range of 21,000 yards.

On March 7th four French battleships temporarily silenced the guns at Dardanus, while two of our ships engaged the guns at Chanak with long-range fire.

On March 10th and 11th the Turkish defences at Bulair and at Morto Bay were bombarded.

On March 11th French warships again shelled the Bulair lines. The Russian Black Sea fleet approached the Bosphorus and sank some Turkish steamers, and also bombarded ports in Asia Minor.

On March 13th General Sir Ian Hamilton, the Commander-in-Chief of the Allied troops in the Mediterranean, received his final instructions from Lord Kitchener.

These instructions were that the army was not to be engaged until the navy had made every effort to force the passage of the Narrows, and that no operations on a large scale were to be undertaken until the 29th Division arrived.

No detailed appreciation of the situation or plan of operations was issued.

On March 15th a light cruiser ran a short way into the Narrows, and was received by heavy fire.

THE DARDANELLES CAMPAIGN 13

Each night minesweepers advanced near the Narrows, guarded by light cruisers and destroyers.

The final and biggest naval attack was made on March 18th with all available battleships.

This was an attempt to force the Narrows by sea power alone. If it failed, it was known that the Narrows would have to be passed with military assistance.

The first bombardment of the sixteen ships engaged on the Allied side against the forts at the Narrows and the batteries protecting the minefields was successful.

The forts at Chanak and Kilid Bahr were first engaged at long range by four British ships. Two British ships engaged the forts at Dardanus, Kephez Point and Soghandere. Four French ships then went close in to the forts to engage them at short range. Six British battleships then made a further bound through the French ships towards Chanak.

The Turks held their fire until the Narrows were full of ships, and then, in addition to the fire from their batteries, they let mines drift down with the current.

Later three battleships were sunk by mines, and the battle cruiser *Inflexible* was severely damaged. Altogether six vessels were put out of action.

The bombardment was continued on both sides during daylight, and then the Allied fleet withdrew.

The attack had failed with a loss of over 2,750 men.

General Liman von Sanders estimated the Turkish loss at 200 men, and the defences had not suffered heavily.

It was realized now that the Narrows could not be forced by ships alone, and that the naval guns were not likely to silence the forts, which have the advantage of concealment and of being a smaller target than a battleship, of which the greater part is vulnerable to shell fire. Observation of fire for land artillery was easy, as the fall of the shells is marked with a splash in the sea if it does not hit its target. It was difficult for guns from ships to obtain the necessary observation for their fire and to elevate their fire sufficiently against shore batteries posted on cliffs rising sheer from the sea. The contest between ships and forts was obviously unequal. The technical, tactical and strategical error of attempting to force the Straits by ships alone had been made clear.

It was now decided that as the navy alone could not force the Straits, the whole army available in the Eastern Mediterranean would have to co-operate. Also the probable result of any further desperate attempts to force the Narrows would have led to the loss of ships, for neither at the Narrows nor at Nagara, three miles north of Chanak, had the forts been silenced.

During the following weeks there were no further naval attacks on a large scale, as the War Council had definitely decided to continue the operations with a combined movement by sea and land.

British submarines, however, were constantly at work in the Straits. On April 17th an attempt was made by the Commander of submarine E. 15 to proceed up the Straits into the Sea of Marmora. Unfortunately, the vessel grounded near Kephez Point. During the night the stranded submarine was torpedoed and rendered useless to the Turks. Gaba Tepe and Enos were repeatedly bombarded in order to cause the Turkish commanders to prepare for landings at these places.

CHAPTER III.

PLAN OF CAMPAIGN.

GENERAL SIR IAN HAMILTON on March 17th arrived at Tenedos, where he was met by Admiral de Robeck, commander of the British fleet, Admiral Guépratte, commander of the French fleet, and General d'Amade, commander of the French Corps. The available Allied forces in the Eastern Mediterranean were as follows: —

The 29th Division, consisting of the 86th, 87th and 88th Brigades.

The Royal Naval Division, consisting of two Naval and one Marine brigades.

The 1st Australian Division, consisting of the 1st New South Wales Brigade, 2nd Victoria Brigade, and the 3rd Brigade, containing a Queensland, a South Australian, a West Australian and a Tasmanian battalion.

The Australian and New Zealand Division, containing the 4th Brigade, the New Zealand Brigade, and the 1st Australian Light Horse Brigade.

The 42nd East Lancashire Division, consisting of the 125th Lancashire Fusilier Brigade, 126th East Lancashire Brigade and the 127th Manchester Brigade.

When active operations started, this 42nd Division and one French division could not be included in the first landing force, as there was not sufficient shipping for them or for one of the French divisions.

The 29th Indian Brigade was also in Egypt.

The French Corps consisted of two divisions each with six batteries of 75's and two mountain batteries. The base of the force was established at Alexandria. There were, however, no first reinforcements of units there and no reserves.

The Turkish forces under General Liman von Sanders were estimated at approximately 45,000 troops with 35,000 in reserve. These forces were distributed as follows: —

5th Division, in the vicinity of Bulair. ⎫ Under Essad Pasha, second in command to
7th Division, in the vicinity of Gallipoli. ⎭ General Liman von Sanders.

9th Division, in the vicinity of Helles.

19th Division, in the vicinity of Maidos and Boghali.

3rd Division, in the vicinity of Kum Kale.

11th Division, in the vicinity of Besika Bay.

In addition, the Turks had available for operations in this area two divisions at Constantinople and nineteen battalions in Asia Minor.

It is now a point for consideration whether the Allied forces were sufficiently strong for their difficult task.

Against the Turkish forces of possibly 80,000, not more than 75,000 were allotted to this campaign by the decision of the War Council on March 28th, and there were immediately available only the 29th Division, the Anzac Corps of two divisions, the Royal Naval Division, and a French division of two brigades.

The reserves, which would not be in the immediate vicinity of the landing operations owing to limitations of shipping resources, would be two Territorial divisions, a French division and an Indian infantry brigade.

It must be noted that the risks would be considerable in view of the strength of the enemy, the difficulties of the country, of obtaining either strategical or tactical surprise at this stage of the operations, and of receiving reinforcements.

The possible landing-places were small and few, and were clearly defined.

Tactical conditions would favour the defence in any disembarkation in face of resistance.

The actual landing on the Peninsula would have little effect, as the Narrows were defended not only by their forts covering the sea route, but by the natural obstacle of the Pasha Dagh running north-west from Kilid Bahr.

Achi Baba with its spurs is a formidable barrier across the south-western end of the Peninsula to a force landing in the vicinity of Cape Helles.

For the capture of these two naturally strong positions land artillery would be required, and also reserves to maintain the momentum of the advance after a landing had been made would have to be at hand.

Neither of these conditions could be fulfilled.

The total force available for the commander was approximately half the strength estimated by Lord Kitchener earlier in the year as necessary for this operation.

Further drawbacks with which the Commander-in-Chief had to grapple were that the Turks were ready for a landing at likely places, and that supplies and water had to be brought overseas, that the country was little known and could not be reconnoitred beforehand by those who would have to operate in it.

In addition, the commencement of his operations was delayed, as he found that his transport had been loaded without

THE DARDANELLES CAMPAIGN

consideration as to the order in which the contents would be wanted.

The ships had to be sent back to Alexandria to be unloaded and reloaded in such a way that the various requirements of the troops would be readily accessible, and to permit a rapid disembarkation on a hostile coast.

That Sir Ian Hamilton realized that his task was not an easy one is evident by his own words in reference to his difficulties; namely, that " no precedent was forthcoming in military history except possibly in the sinister legends of Xerxes."

The delay in reloading the transports added to his difficulties, as the Turks had further weeks in which to strengthen and conceal their positions.

For the possible success of this operation, however, it was essential to act quickly as soon as it was started.

Sir Ian Hamilton reported that " nothing but a thorough and systematic scheme for flinging the whole of the troops under my command very rapidly ashore could be expected to meet with success."

For this it was essential that the weapons, munitions and equipment should be ready to be unloaded in the required order of precedence.

The transports had to be reloaded at Alexandria in such a manner as to permit a rapid disembarkation to be made.

It was not until April 23rd that they were back at the required starting-points of the embarking troops.

By this time the Turks at the landing-places chosen for our troops were distributed as follows:—

> One battalion was at the toe of the Peninsula.
> One battalion was on the Kum Kale coast.
> One company was at the beach selected for the landing of the Anzac Corps, with another company in close support.
> Two battalions with a mountain battery were in reserve in this area.

It was estimated that, in all, there were seventeen Turkish battalions at this time between Suvla and Sedd-el-Bahr, and twenty-one in the northern part of the Peninsula.

The courses then open to the Commander-in-Chief were:—

> (a) To attack the Bulair lines.
> (b) To land at Enos.
> (c) To land on the Asiatic coast.
> (d) To land on the Gallipoli Peninsula.

The landing-places on the Peninsula were limited to Helles, Gaba Tepe, Suvla Bay and Aja Liman Bay (six miles north-east of Suvla Bay).

Sir Ian Hamilton decided in favour of two main landings to be made on the Peninsula, and part of one available French division was, in addition, to land at Kum Kale as a subsidiary operation to neutralize Turkish troops and guns, which might otherwise be employed at Helles.

The main reasons for selecting the fourth of the above-mentioned courses were that: —

- (a) The flanks of the landing force at Helles could be protected by the Navy.
- (b) The landing-place was sheltered.
- (c) On first landing there would not be an extended front to hold and its flanks would be secured.

The main drawbacks to landing at five different points at Helles were: —

- (a) That there was dispersion of force in proximity to the enemy in country where intercommunication was very difficult.
- (b) That the enemy were guarding the landing-places.
- (c) That the distance to the Narrows was greater than from Gaba Tepe.
- (d) That all the force could have been disembarked together within a few hours with the available shipping at and north of Gaba Tepe; thus avoiding dispersion of force.
- (e) That by landing the whole force at and north of Gaba Tepe there would have been every prospect of quickly and successfully capturing Sari Bair, an important step on the road to the Narrows.
- (f) That by landing at the toe of the Peninsula formidable heights would still have to be surmounted before the Narrows could be dominated by land.
- (g) That the country between Cape Helles and the Narrows favours the defenders, as the ravines are at right angles to the line of advance, and the country gradually rises from the sea where Hills 114, 138 and 141 dominate the landing-places up to Achi Baba, which is 709 feet at its highest point.

However, there never has been and never will be perfection in military or other plans. Our Regulations have some comforting words to say on this subject. We all know that

THE DARDANELLES CAMPAIGN

mortals cannot command success; they can only try to deserve it.

In these operations the efforts of Commander-in-Chief, his Staff and all those under his command certainly deserved the success which they just failed to obtain.

The details of the plan were that the 29th Division was to land at Helles supported by the Royal Naval Division and later reinforced by the French troops, which were to land at Kum Kale.

The landing at Gaba Tepe was to be carried out by the Anzac Corps under General Sir William Birdwood.

Feints were to be made in the Gulf of Saros at the Bulair Lines by a part of the Royal Naval Division to mystify the enemy as to the intentions of the Allies.

The result of these plans and preparations was that after dark on April 24th transports were taking fifty-three battalions to their rendezvous for the landing operations on the following day.

The French troops were steaming towards Kum Kale, the troops from Tenedos were on the way to Helles; from Imbros the Anzac Corps were being taken towards Gaba Tepe and part of the Royal Naval Division towards the Gulf of Saros.

CHAPTER IV.

THE LANDINGS.

SOON after daybreak on April 25th the Royal Naval Division arrived at their rendezvous in the Gulf of Saros.

The Bulair Lines were then bombarded and demonstrations were made by troops embarking in boats, which were towed towards the shore. After dark the troops returned to the transports.

LANDING AT ANZAC.

The Anzac Corps was to be landed two thousand yards north of Gaba Tepe on a front of 1,600 yards.

The orders for this Corps were to advance on Maidos with a view to cutting the Turkish communications. Actually, the Corps arrived on either side of Ari Burnu on a front of 1,100 yards, a mile north of the beach at Gaba Tepe, which had been the selected landing-place. The battleships *Queen*, *London* and *Prince of Wales* carried the troops to within a short distance of the beach. The covering troops then got into forty-eight boats. They were landed in two trips within half an hour of each other. The first trip reached the beach at 0425 hours.

The beach on which the landing took place was under the precipitous cliffs of the Sari Bair spurs. This was fortunate at first, as, although the steepness of the cliffs was a serious obstacle, yet there were only a few defenders in the trenches on the beach and the side of the cliffs, so that the high ground overlooking the landing-place was secured at the first assault.

The first objective for the covering force, consisting of the 3rd Australian Infantry Brigade, the 1st Field Company, R.E., and the bearer sub-divisions of the 3rd Field Ambulances, was to occupy Chunuk Bair.

The 2nd Brigade, on landing after the covering party, was to extend the left flank of the 3rd Brigade to include Hill 971 and to protect the left flank by holding a line to include Fisherman's Hut.

The Turks in the vicinity of Ari Burnu were completely surprised by the arrival of the 3rd Australian Brigade. There was only some erratic firing from the posts overlooking the beach where the landing took place.

On arrival at the top of the cliffs, however, the Turks brought effective flanking fire to bear from their guns at Gaba

THE DARDANELLES CAMPAIGN

Tepe on to the troops, on to the beach and on to the ships and boats.

Units had become mixed up during the landing, and so reorganization of units when Plugge's Plateau, at the summit of the cliffs, was reached, caused considerable delay. Also, owing to the error in the landing of the covering party the 2nd Brigade had to be directed to try to rectify matters by operating on the right instead of on the left of the 3rd Brigade.

By 0700 hours advanced parties of the covering force had reached positions nearly two miles from the sea, and points twelve hundred yards east of the landing-place had definitely been gained. The intricate nature of the country now made it very difficult for commanders to appreciate the situation on their own front. Had there been less disintegration of units in the landing, and had the country been less difficult, there is little doubt that the 8,000 Anzac troops, who had disembarked by 0840 hours, could have established themselves on Chunuk Bair before the arrival of Mustapha Kemal Bey with his 19th Division.

The first Turks, opposing the landing up to 0800 hours, consisted of a battalion on a five-mile front, with outpost companies on the coast. Mustapha Kemal's advanced troops did not get into touch with the advanced parties of the landing troops until 1000 hours.

By 1400 hours the 1st and 2nd Brigades and two mountain batteries had reinforced the 3rd Australian Brigade. However, by this time a great deal of the advantage gained by the initial dashing attack had been lost. Many small and isolated parties had endeavoured to exploit the initial success and were cut off.

By 1500 hours the Turkish 19th Division had concentrated in the vicinity of the Anzac's position. Soon after 1600 hours the Turks counter-attacked and captured Hill 700.

By 1800 hours, 15,000 of all ranks had been landed and a position was established covering the landing-place, and all counter-attacks had been driven off.

The Anzacs were able to consolidate a semi-circular position on a front of approximately two miles, with their right flank about a mile north of Gaba Tepe and their left flank on the high ground above Fisherman's Hut.

The situation was, however, not satisfactory. There had been heavy losses. There was no depth to the position. Ammunition was running short; water was scarce in this area. The landing-place was exposed in the event of bad weather, and so there would always be difficulties in bringing reinforcements and supplies up the steep and open gradients behind the position which the Anzacs had taken up.

There was no hope at present of getting into touch with the troops who had landed at Helles. The question of withdrawal was even considered by General Birdwood and his divisional commanders. Instructions were, however, received from Sir Ian Hamilton to maintain positions on the ground gained at all costs.

This quick decision showed at the outset of the operations the Commander-in-Chief's resolution, which was so valuable and prominent during the campaign, inspiring the troops and their leaders to hold positions in which the Turks had all the advantage of observation and field of fire.

During the following months the Anzac troops caused heavy losses in the Turkish ranks and contained at close quarters equal numbers to their own, and in addition caused them to keep strong reserves about Maidos. Had they been able to capture a more extended area when they first arrived at the summit of the cliffs their task subsequently would have been much easier. Had the tactical importance of Pine Ridge, Lone Pine Plateau, The Nek and Baby been realized, and if they had been secured, their occupation would have saved many casualties. The eagerness and gallantry of the Anzac troops led to their later troubles.

The first parties who landed and dashed ahead unsupported into the hilly, tangled country towards Sari Bair were no doubt anxious to carry out the sound principle of gaining as much depth to the position on first landing before the enemy could concentrate against the point where their unexpected landing had taken place. It must be emphasized, however, that the first consignment of troops was deflected so far from the intended landing-place that the covering force was thrown into confusion and higher command then had added difficulties in controlling operations. Had, however, cohesion in the ranks been maintained, the spirit animating their isolated raiders would have been turned to valuable account.

The great difficulties of operating over unknown, intricate ground without adequate artillery support would in a great measure have been overcome, as an ample area of ground might have been occupied and consolidated before the enemy's reinforcements could arrive. Such an opportunity could never recur.

Landing at Helles.

The landings in this area were made at five different beaches by twelve and a half battalions. The conditions varied considerably at each beach. From east to west the beaches were named " S," " V," " W," " X " and " Y."

THE DARDANELLES CAMPAIGN

" S " Beach was at Eski-Hissarlik Point.
" V " Beach was between Sedd-el-Bahr and Cape Helles.
Camber Beach, which was part of " V " Beach, was directly below Sedd-el-Bahr.
" W " Beach was at Cape Helles and Cape Tekke.
" X " Beach was 1,000 yards north-east of Cape Tekke.
" Y " Beach was 7,000 yards north-east of Cape Tekke.

The Turks in the Helles area on the morning of April 25th, when the landing took place, were two battalions and a company of Engineers.

Actually at the beaches their outposts were as follows: at " S " Beach they had one forward platoon with a company in the vicinity; at " V " and " W " Beaches they had two companies; at " X " Beach there were twelve men; and at " Y " Beach the landing was unopposed. The nearest Turks in this area were two platoons near Gully Ravine.

The landings at " V," " W " and " X " Beaches were to be the main operation; those at " S " and " Y " were intended to protect the flanks.

The objective was the capture of Achi Baba.

At " S " Beach the 2nd Bn. The South Wales Borderers (less one company) and a detachment of the 2nd London Field Company, R.E., made the landing. It was not effected until 0730 hours owing to the strong current, but then the high ground near de Tott's Battery was soon captured with the help of the covering fire from the ships.

The force at " S " Beach was out of touch with any of the other detachments that landed on April 25th. It was therefore important to do more than maintain its position and wait until the other troops at " V " and " W " Beaches were able to advance.

However, in accordance with orders, the commander of this landing party remained in his position and consolidated it, as reports had been received that the Turks were in force in the vicinity, and he did not feel justified in not conforming strictly to his orders.

From a review of the situation now, it is apparent that intervention on the part of the South Wales Borderers on the flank of the Turks opposing the landing at " V " Beach would have been most effective.

" Y " Beach.

The 1st Bn. The King's Own Scottish Borderers, the Plymouth Battalion, R.M.L.I., and a company of the 2nd Bn. The South Wales Borderers were successfully landed covered by fire from

H.M.S. *Goliath*. The troops reached the top of the high cliffs overlooking the beach without opposition.

The Turks were not watching this landing-place, as they evidently considered that such difficult country did not require defence.

The co-operation of the force landed at " Y " Beach against the flank of the troops opposing the landings farther south would have been most valuable. The orders, however, given to the commander of this force did not definitely state that in the event of the advance from the south not being possible there should be any further action on his part.

The stout resistance offered by the troops at " Y " Beach in repulsing night and dawn attacks on April 26th contained one and a half Turkish battalions for twenty-nine hours.

On April 26th the troops at " Y " Beach, with all wounded and stores, were removed, covered by the fire of the warships. Had the troops at " Y " Beach advanced or had they been reinforced and given a definite co-ordinated task with the troops landing farther south, a junction with these troops might easily have been effected and the whole situation so much improved for the troops at the main landings, that the objective allotted for them might have been captured. As it was, the commander waited for an advance from the southern beaches. When this advance did not take place the commander waited for further orders. These orders did not arrive. Had the reinforcements from the Divisional reserve been sent to " Y " Beach with direct orders how to co-operate with the troops at " X " and " W " Beaches, the Turks would have been forced to evacuate Hill 138 and Sedd-el-Bahr and the whole of the initial landing operation might have been successful.

For the main landings at " V," " W " and " X " Beaches the first objective was to be the capture of the high ground dominating these beaches.

The second objective was to occupy a line from Sedd-el-Bahr to " Y " Beach. The whole force was then to advance on Achi Baba.

Landing at " V " Beach.

" V " Beach was protected by three strong lines of wire entanglement extending into the sea and covered by a network of concealed trenches. It consisted of a strip of beach 350 yards long and ten yards wide. The ground from the beach sloped gradually up to the cliff 100 feet above. The flanks were strongly guarded by the ruins of the old fort and village of Sedd-el-Bahr on the east, and by perpendicular cliffs on the west.

THE DARDANELLES CAMPAIGN 25

The largest force had been detailed to land at this beach, as its capture was of primary importance in the general scheme.

At " V " Beach the Munster Fusiliers, two companies of the Hampshire Regiment, one company of the Dublin Fusiliers and a Field Company, R.E., were conveyed in a collier, the *River Clyde*. This ship had been specially prepared for the disembarkation of troops. Large doors had been cut in her sides, and gangways had been constructed, so that troops could reach the lighters, which were to be grounded ahead between the *River Clyde* and the shore to form a bridge to the beach.

Three companies of Royal Dublin Fusiliers were to be towed ashore, of which half a company were to land at Camber Beach east of Sedd-el-Bahr.

" V " Beach and Sedd-el-Bahr were subjected to a heavy bombardment from the *Cornwallis, Albion* and *Queen Elizabeth*. Then the first boat-loads, towed by steam pinnaces, attempted to land. They were met by very heavy rifle and machine-gun fire, which was not opened till the boats had cast off from the steam pinnaces. The few men of the first trip who were not killed were able to find some shelter under a bank of sand five feet high on the beach. The landing party was unable to advance beyond this bank during daylight.

As soon as the boats with the three companies of the Royal Dublin Fusiliers had reached the beach, the *River Clyde* was run ashore towards the eastern end of the beach. Unfortunately, the *River Clyde* grounded earlier and in deeper water than had been anticipated, and so there was great difficulty in bringing the lighters into positions to form a bridge between the ship and the shore. This difficulty was accentuated by the strong current.

The lighters which were to form the bridge to the shore were run out ahead, but unfortunately too far, so that a gap was left between two lighters.

As soon as the doors in the steel side of the collier were opened, very heavy fire was poured on to the two hundred men who came out in an attempt to land.

By 1100 hours nearly a thousand men had left the cover of the ship and tried to get ashore, but owing to their heavy losses the disembarkation was stopped. The remainder of the men in the *River Clyde* remained in her until after nightfall, when they were able to land.

The machine guns in the *River Clyde* saved the landing at this beach from complete disaster by keeping down the fire directed on the men who had landed and were partially sheltered by the sand-bank on the beach.

The troops at " V " Beach were, however, isolated, as

neither flank detachment at " S " and " W " Beaches had been able to get into touch with them.

A night attack on the Turks' position in the old fort and village of Sedd-el-Bahr failed. The reason for this was that our troops were exhausted, and the Turks' position had not been definitely located. Bright moonlight in addition gave the defenders every advantage.

Landing at Camber Beach.

A half-company of the Royal Dublin Fusiliers was landed at Camber Beach without opposition. Their further advance was only possible on a narrow front.

After several attempts to enter Sedd-el-Bahr the troops had to withdraw after suffering a heavy proportion of casualties.

Landing at " W " Beach.

This beach consisted of a sandy strip 350 yards long up to 40 yards wide. It was commanded by sloping cliffs offering excellent positions for trenches with effective fire on to the landing-places. The only point where it was possible to get immunity from the defenders' fire on landing at " W " Beach was at a small ledge of rock under the cliff at Cape Tekke.

The Turks had strengthened their position with land and sea mines and a broad wire entanglement stretching into the sea along the whole front of the beach.

The 1st Bn. The Lancashire Fusiliers were brought in H.M.S. *Euryalus* to positions near the landing-place where the troops were embarked in the boats at 0400 hours. At 0500 hours the supporting ships bombarded the beach and the Turkish positions farther north. At 0600 hours the Lancashire Fusiliers were landed in three groups.

The troops landing on the rocks at Cape Tekke were able to rush with the bayonet the enemy's machine guns concealed in the cliffs, and they thus enfiladed the Turkish main position.

The troops who were landed nearest to Cape Helles, though losing heavily, pressed forward through the barbed wire and gained possession of the beach and the approaches to it.

At 0930 hours the Worcestershires were landed on the rocks at Cape Tekke. They then advanced towards Hill 114 on the southern side of which a party of the Lancashire Fusiliers had been checked.

By midday Hill 114 had been captured by combined offensive operations with the 7th Royal Fusiliers, who had landed at " X " Beach.

The Worcestershires then co-operated with the third group of the Lancashire Fusiliers, who had landed west of Hill 138.

THE DARDANELLES CAMPAIGN

By 1400 hours the ground leading to Hill 138 had been sufficiently cleared of wire by bombardment from the sea to enable an advance to be made.

By 1600 hours the Worcestershires and Lancashire Fusiliers had captured this hill and one of the redoubts on it. Had they been able to capture the second redoubt on Hill 138 a general advance might have been made at " W " Beach. This operation would have enabled the troops at " V " Beach to work their way forward.

Unfortunately, the commander of the 88th Brigade had been killed; the Divisional Commander was on board ship and so was not in close touch with the situation on land. Only by his direct orders could the Divisional reserve of two battalions at " X " Beach have been used, and so it can now be seen that an opportunity was missed of capturing Hill 138 at the first attempt and so of gaining a considerable success.

An unsuccessful attempt was then made to join up with the troops on " V " Beach.

Landing at " X " Beach.

Under cover of the guns of the *Implacable* and *Swiftsure* the 2nd Royal Fusiliers landed by 0515 hours on the morning of April 25th without loss. Their objective was to capture Hill 114 and to join up with the Lancashire Fusiliers at " W " Beach. The enemy, however, were found to be in a strong position on Hill 114, and the enemy's heavy artillery from the vicinity of Krithia had the range of the ground west of Hill 114.

Reinforced later by the Border Regiment and Inniskilling Fusiliers, the Royal Fusiliers were able to join up with the Lancashire Fusiliers and entrench on a line from their landing-place to Hill 114, where the line was extended through Hill 138 to just east of Cape Helles' ruined lighthouse.

The reasons why a further advance was not made in this area between Cape Helles and " X " Beach were that reserves were not available at the points where success had been gained, and that success was not exploited at " S " and " Y " on our first arrival at these beaches.

It was also very difficult for the commander of the Helles landing operations to collect and then to collate the information received from troops at five landing-places, especially as two brigade commanders and two brigade majors were early put out of action.

Landing at Kum Kale.

The landing of the French force under General d'Amade was successfully carried out. The orders to General d'Amade for his landing at Kum Kale on the Asiatic coast were to send an infantry regiment, a field battery and a section of Engineers to clear the enemy from the area, Yeni Shehr—Kum Kale—both inclusive up to the River Mendere.

There was little opposition at Kum Kale owing to the effective shelling by the three supporting battleships and three cruisers. After the preliminary bombardment by the ships the French troops began to land at 1000 hours. By the early afternoon the whole force was ashore.

Their primary object was effectively carried out by capturing the Kum Kale Fort and preventing the enemy's guns from bringing fire to bear on the ships off Cape Helles or on to the troops during their landing operations. When, however, their columns attempted to carry out an advance along the coast to Yeni Shehr, they were met by such heavy fire from the Turks in trenches south of Kum Kale that their further advance was checked and had to be discontinued during the day. During the night, Turkish counter-attacks were repulsed.

The losses of the French during this operation were 788 casualties, but they captured 400 prisoners and materially assisted in the landing of our troops at Helles on April 25th.

CHAPTER V.

First Battle of Krithia.

The result of the landing operations by the morning of April 26th was that only a precarious lodgment had been gained on the fringe of the coast.

Progress, however, was made on April 26th, and a foothold was obtained across the southern end of the Peninsula. By the evening a continuous line was held from the north of Sedd-el-Bahr to " X " Beach.

At " V " Beach, the fresh troops landed during the night attacked Hill 141 after a bombardment by the fleet.

The Turks in the vicinity of this hill and the ruins of Sedd-el-Bahr were estimated at three companies.

After considerable fighting in Sedd-el-Bahr, Hill 141 was captured by 1430 hours, and touch with the Lancashire Fusiliers was obtained.

The position was now consolidated. The Turks, on the other hand, were retiring on Krithia. Had reinforcements been available at this period to press forward with the troops at Sedd-el-Bahr and " S " Beach valuable ground might have been gained.

More infantry were landed at " W " and " X " Beaches during April 26th.

General d'Amade reported that owing to the Turks being reinforced at Kum Kale no further progress could be made unless the rest of the French Division could be landed.

As troops were urgently required at " W " Beach, it was decided to withdraw the French detachment from Kum Kale. This was carried out without loss under cover of darkness.

On the Anzac Front on April 26th there was heavy fighting between 0930 hours and noon.

An attempt by the 4th Australian Battalion to advance into No Man's Land on 400' Plateau led to heavy casualties.

A line was consolidated on this front from Brighton Beach through Bolton's Ridge, 400' Plateau, Maclaurin's Hill, Quinn's Post, Pope's Hill, Walker's Ridge to North Beach. The length of line was approximately one and a half miles. The greatest depth of the position from the sea was a thousand yards. The Turks had all the advantages of observation and field of fire up to the anchorages behind the Anzac position.

On April 27th, at 1600 hours, there was a general advance on the Helles front. The Turkish 9th Division offered weak resistance, so that by 1730 hours a new line had been occupied, joining up with the troops above "S" Beach on the right.

This new line, approximately three miles long, was from Eski Hissarlik to a point 500 yards south of Gully Ravine. There was a definite salient in this line at the point where it joined the right of the 87th Brigade in the vicinity of Kirte Dere.

As, however, troops were much exhausted, and as there was a shortage of gun teams and of animals for the twenty-eight guns that had been landed, and as the adequate supply of water and food was still a problem, the further advance towards Achi Baba was postponed.

The whole of the 29th Division and some French battalions were ashore on April 27th.

It was necessary to gain more depth to the position at Helles, to obtain fresh water supplies, and to improve the tactical situation. It was decided, therefore, to continue offensive operations on the following day.

The first objectives were to be an advance on a two-mile front on the left flank up to Hill 472; then there was to be a general advance towards Hill 236, near de Totts' Battery, and the mouth of Gully Ravine, to be continued to Krithia and Achi Baba.

The Turks now had been reinforced by four battalions, and had approximately eight battalions on this front, with two in reserve near Krithia.

Our general advance began soon after the bombardment of Krithia and Achi Baba had started. Our line was held by the 29th Division (less two battalions) on the left and centre. On the right of the 29th Division were three French battalions.

For the first hour the advance of the 29th Division progressed satisfactory. Later the resistance increased, and the Turks made strong counter-attacks, especially at the point of junction between the 88th Brigade, on the right of the 29th Division, and the left of the French troops.

The reserve brigade of the 29th Division was sent forward at 1300 hours to endeavour to pass through the 88th Brigade and reach Krithia. The majority of this brigade was unable to advance beyond the line held by the 88th Brigade. The French, on their right, were forced to withdraw by heavy pressure directed at this point by Turkish reinforcements.

By this time all our available troops, except the Drake Battalion, Royal Naval Division were in the forward positions. Ammunition supply was becoming reduced.

The strain on officers and men of the sleepless nights and heavy fighting of the past few days began to tell. The casualties in the ranks of both the French battalions and the 29th Division were considerable, and though the Turkish casualties had been heavy, too, this was unknown at the time. The result was that about a mile of ground was gained and consolidated by 1800 hours.

Achi Baba, the objective for the troops at Helles, was out of reach for the present. With reference to this situation, Sir Ian Hamilton, in his despatches, wrote as follows:—" The men were exhausted, and the few guns landed at the time were unable to afford them adequate artillery support. The small amount of ammunition did not suffice to maintain the supply of munitions, and cartridges were running short, despite all efforts to push them up from the landing place. Had it been possible to push in reinforcements in men, artillery and munitions during the day, Krithia should have fallen, and much subsequent fighting for its capture would have been avoided. Two days later this would have been feasible, but I had to reckon with the certainty that the enemy would, in that same time, have received proportionately greater support."

During the night the gaps in our original line were filled up, and the disorganization in units caused during the day's fighting was satisfactory rectified. It was evident, however, that now the British plan had failed. No reinforcements were immediately available. The Turkish positions were daily becoming more formidable, and reinforcements were being brought into the area of operations from Smyrna and Constantinople.

The battle of the landing ended on April 28th, and little more than a landing had been effected at a loss of over ten thousand men.

It had failed in its objects, which were to make a junction between the troops landing at Helles and at Gaba Tepe, to capture Krithia and Achi Baba and to advance upon Maidos and the Narrows.

The chief causes for this result were that the attacks were delivered in insufficient force; there were no reserves available on the spot; the lack of topographical knowledge caused the forces available to be unduly dispersed during the landing, and the element of surprise was eliminated owing to the original decision to rely on naval strength alone to capture the Dardanelles.

The original strategical decision had been made without sufficient consideration of the tactical difficulties involved.

Those who planned the campaign did not realize that sea power alone was insufficient to cause the defeat of a Continental army, for the War Council, on January 13th, 1915, decided that the Admiralty should undertake the capture of the Gallipoli Peninsula.

Sir Ian Hamilton received scanty information as to the requirements. His units were sent to the area of operations without their first reinforcements. General Liman von Sanders had adequate time after the Admiralty started operations to strengthen and man his defences sufficiently to prevent the objectives in our landing from being attained.

A point for consideration is whether it would have been better to have used all the troops for one landing. As it was, there were no reserves at either Helles or Anzac.

Reinforcements of four battalions of the Royal Naval Division had to be sent to assist the Anzac Corps, whose units were scattered and depleted.

Had General Birdwood's suggestion to withdraw from Anzac Cove been adopted, his corps would have been available for the capture of Krithia and Achi Baba. As it was, the attack at Helles on April 28th had to be carried out by troops exhausted by fighting, want of sleep and water, and by the hard work of landing ammunition and stores.

Not only the necessary reserves of man power would have been available, but also the much-needed artillery support would have been increased.

The question of the difficulty of artillery support is clearly dealt with in Sir Ian Hamilton's despatch of December 11th, 1915: "Normally it may be correct to say that in modern war infantry cannot be expected to advance without artillery preparation. But in a landing on a hostile shore this order has to be inverted. The infantry must advance and seize a suitable position to cover the landing and provide artillery positions for the main thrust. The very existence of the force . . . must absolutely depend on the infantry being able instantly to make good sufficient ground without the aid of artillery other than can be supplied for the purpose of floating batteries."

On April 28th the supporting artillery and ammunition was limited; the ground was cut up by ravines, which were unknown, and so could not be indicated to the supporting naval guns.

The conclusion may be reached that had fresh troops and additional artillery and ammunition been available for the attack at Helles on April 28th the operation might have been successful.

The state of affairs at Helles on this day was not so difficult as at Gaba Tepe, where the available reserves were required only to establish the situation on the Anzac front; whereas at Helles all could have co-operated in an attack on the enemy checking our advance on Achi Baba and Krithia.

The advantage of numbers would have been on our side, even if all the Turks from the vicinity of Anzac had concentrated at Helles.

One point had been clearly brought out in the fighting of the past few days with reference to the idea that Turkish resistance would be slight if the attacks were vigorously pressed.

It had been a delusion to imagine that the Turks would not defend stoutly and counter-attack resolutely if an attempt was made to drive them out of positions on their own soil.

CHAPTER VI.

Second Battle of Krithia.

On the two days following the attack on April 28th, the work of straightening our line and consolidating it was continued with little interference from the Turks.

More artillery was landed and local reserves were formed at Helles.

On May 1st the 29th Indian Brigade arrived and was placed in reserve. At 2200 hours on this day, before moonrise, the Turks advanced. Their first assault was against the centre of the position held by the 29th Division. The 7th and 9th Turkish Divisions were successful at first in gaining a footing in a part of the front line trenches on the French left, where Singalese troops had been holding the line.

A company of the Worcestershire Regiment, reinforced later by a battalion of the Royal Naval Division, restored the situation, after considerable fighting, by 0200 hours. The Turks lost heavily during their attacks.

At 0500 hours a counter-attack was made on the whole front and the line advanced.

On the left, within two and a half hours, the 29th Division had gained 500 yards. On the right the enemy had strong positions in the Kereves Dere, and as no progress was possible in this area the troops, who had advanced in the centre and on the left, came under heavy enfilade machine-gun fire. Owing to the resistance on their front they could not hold the positions won. The whole force then withdrew to its original line of trenches, having captured 350 prisoners.

Our losses up to date totalled 177 officers and 1,990 killed, 8,219 wounded, and 130 officers and 3,580 other ranks missing.

The Turks attacked again on the nights of May 2nd-3rd and 3rd-4th with eight battalions against the portion of the line held by the French. These attacks were repulsed with heavy loss.

On May 2nd the 87th Brigade advanced east of Gully Ravine and captured a Turkish trench and 123 prisoners.

The attempt by the French troops to capture the strong positions on the high ground above Kereves Dere was unsuccessful.

At Anzac on this day orders were issued for operations to be undertaken on the front of the Anzac Corps to improve the position on Hill 700. This was to be carried out by three battalions. Owing to the difficulties of the ground and of night operations, and owing to a miscalculation by one battalion of time and distance, causing it to arrive at the rendezvous one and a half hours too late there was no gain of ground. The attacking battalions lost 600 men.

At Suvla fifty New Zealanders were landed at Suvla Bay. They occupied Lala Baba and captured an officer and twelve men.

On May 5th the Lancashire Fusilier Brigade (5th, 6th, 7th and 8th Lancashire Fusiliers) of the 42nd Territorial Division was disembarked from Egypt and posted in reserve at Helles.

Preparations for a fresh attempt to advance at Helles were now made. The 2nd Australian Brigade and the New Zealand Brigade from Anzac embarked for operations in the Helles area. Preparations for a fresh attempt to advance at Helles had now been made.

The second battle of Krithia was fought on May 6th, 7th and 8th. The immediate object was to gain ground between the opposing trenches, and then to seize Krithia, Achi Baba and the high ground across the peninsula five miles from its extremity.

After the first battle of Krithia, Sir Ian Hamilton had been able to create a reserve consisting of two Anzac brigades and two battalions of the Royal Naval Division.

One brigade of the Royal Naval Division was allotted to the French Corps.

At 1100 hours on May 6th the attack started with the advance of the 88th Brigade of the 29th Division towards Fir Tree Wood. Here our troops were held up by the Turks' machine guns.

The advance throughout the front was not simultaneous with the result that advancing troops had their flanks exposed and could not exploit their successes. All the troops were tired and little artillery support with high explosive shells was available.

The French started their attack against the Turks' position on the ridge above the valley, through which the Kereves Dere runs, supported by their 75's from the vicinity of Sedd-el-Bahr.

On the left the Turks' forward posts were captured, but their main positions were not reached.

In the first two hours' fighting the centre of our line had been advanced four hundred yards, and in many other parts up to three hundred yards.

During the next three hours' fighting, in which there were many counter-attacks, there was no material addition to our gains.

Orders were then given to consolidate the positions gained.

On the right the French reached the crest overlooking the Kereves Dere, but the Turks' fire was so accurately ranged on to this mark that they could proceed no further.

During the night they were able to repulse a bayonet attack.

On the second day of the Krithia battle the naval guns directed their fire against the Turkish positions near Krithia and in front of our left flank.

At 0945 hours the artillery carried out a preliminary bombardment, but owing to the extensive area to be covered by the limited number of guns and owing to the shortage of ammunition it was not effective.

At 1000 hours the Lancashire Fusilier Brigade started the attack. They were met by such heavy fire from machine guns that had not been silenced, that progress was very slow and losses were heavy.

Soon after midday our advance was brought to a standstill after the Lancashire Fusilier Brigade had been reinforced on their right flank by the 87th Brigade and Fir Tree Wood on this flank had been captured by a battalion of the 88th Brigade.

The Turks counter-attacked vigorously during the afternoon.

On the front of the French troops the Turks had strengthened their positions, so that there was no general progress as a result of their attacks.

At 1645 hours the attack was renewed and the whole line advanced. Except on the extreme left progress was made.

The Turks, however, had brought fresh guns into action and General d'Amade had to use up his reserves in order to restore the situation on his part of the line.

The general attack was renewed on the British front at 1810 hours, but there was only a limited success.

It was necessary then to consolidate the ground gained. This was done with little interference from the Turks during the night.

The New Zealand Brigade replaced the Lancashire Fusilier Brigade which went into reserve.

Sir Ian Hamilton decided to continue the offensive, as he knew that fresh Turkish reinforcements (the 2nd, 4th, 13th, 15th and 16th Divisions) were at hand, and if the objectives were to be gained there was no time to lose.

The naval bombardment began soon after 100 hours, but it was apparent when the attack started that there had been little result from it.

At 1030 hours the New Zealand and 87th Brigades began to advance.

They were met by machine-gun and rifle fire, which was

THE DARDANELLES CAMPAIGN 37

just as heavy as had been met by the Lancashire Fusilier brigade on the day before.

After much hard fighting the greatest advance was to a depth of three hundred yards by 1330 hours.

The French reported that they could not advance unless the British line went further forward.

There was then a long pause in the operations.

At 1600 hours Sir Ian Hamilton ordered a general advance as a final effort to be made on Krithia at 1730 hours preceded by a bombardment.

The general advance was carried out, and more ground was gained, but the Turks' main position was unbroken.

By 1900 hours our final effort had definitely failed and orders were issued for the positions to be consolidated. This was the last phase of the second battle of Krithia.

Our two main forces at Helles and Anzac had not been linked up, and there was little hope now of capturing Krithia and Achi Baba by direct assault.

During the past three days there had been thirty per cent. casualties of the troops engaged, this was at a rate of a thousand casualties per hundred yards of advance owing to the enemy's effective machine-gun fire and our limited artillery support.

The ammunition shortage was due to the requirements for our intended offensive on the Western Front at Aubers Ridge and Festubert.

We had not in Britain the available trained men, guns and ammunition for two great offensives, both at Gallipoli and in France; therefore, both offensives failed.

It would have been better to have appreciated the general situation and to have decided where to utilize the available resources in men, guns and ammunition. The War Council could then have made a decision between the conflicting claims of the two areas of operation.

As it was, the lack of success of our May offensives in France was due to shortage of artillery ammunition; which also was an important factor in preventing the troops at Helles from capturing their main objectives.

Hopes of reaching the Narrows with the depleted forces and limited ammunition available now disappeared.

The strength of the Turks' positions, their armament and numbers were realized. They were in strong positions; our beaches and piers were overlooked, and were under effective gun fire.

Bad weather would make the landing of ammunition and stores impossible.

Sir Ian Hamilton reported that operations had reached " the limit of what could be attained by mingling initiative with surprise. Siege warfare was soon bound to supersede manœuvre battles in the open. Consolidation and fortification of our front, improvement of approaches, selection of machine-gun emplacements, and scientific grouping of our artillery under a centralized control must ere long form the tactical basis of our plans."

During this battle at Helles the Anzac troops had been carrying out their rôle of containing as large a body of the enemy as possible in order to relieve the situation on the front of the French and 29th Divisions.

A series of attacks and counter-attacks were made between May 6th and 11th, but neither side could make any real impression on the main position held by the other.

The Turks held naturally strong positions against which our frontal attacks and our present positions at Helles could be observed and fired on at will.

They were helped by German leadership and scientific skill. German submarines were reported to be in the Mediterranean.

Our casualties had been approximately 14,000.

Nor was our force of 20,000 men at Helles strong enough to attack a nearly equal force in a prepared position.

Owing to the offensive operations in France during May sufficient men were not available to enable Sir Ian Hamilton to capture either Achi Baba or Chunuk Bair.

Had the offensives in France not been undertaken, and had the Gallipoli campaign been fully supported with all available resources it is more than possible that success would have been the result.

Work was now carried out in organizing the areas and their communications and landing-places.

CHAPTER VII.

OPERATIONS UP TO END OF JUNE.

THE Helles front was now divided into four sectors, held from right to left as follows:—

(1) On the right by French troops.
(2) On the right centre by the Royal Naval Division.
(3) On the left centre was the 42nd Division.
(4) On the left were the 29th Division and 29th Indian Infantry Brigade.

These troops formed the VIII Corps. Trench warfare now began.

On May 12th a strong Turkish redoubt north-east of Beach "Y" was captured by the 6th Gurkhas after dark, and the line on this flank was advanced five hundred yards.

The Turks were completely surprised by this attack, which was made possible by the wonderful climbing abilities of the Gurkhas, who were able to scale the almost precipitous cliffs from the beach.

At 1830 hours on May 12th two cruisers bombarded the Turkish lines near the objective, assisted by the 29th Divisional Artillery.

The Manchester Brigade of the 42nd Division co-operated with machine gun and rifle fire from their trenches to distract the Turks' attention from any flank attack.

The leading company of Gurkhas, on forming up at the top of the cliffs, rushed the Turkish redoubt. This company was followed by another which helped to consolidate the position gained. The total losses in this raid were twenty-one killed and ninety-two wounded.

On May 13th Lord Kitchener reported to the War Council that all available troops that could be spared from England were required in France.

The considerations then for the War Council were whether (a) the Gallipoli campaign should be abandoned; (b) only the 52nd Division, promised as a reinforcement, should be sent, and that with the available forces Sir Ian Hamilton should endeavour to make a slow advance towards the Narrows; (c) all available forces should be sent to the Peninsula for further attacks on the Turkish position.

The situation in the Peninsula was not promising, and might reasonably at this juncture have prompted the War Council to decide on abandoning the Gallipoli campaign.

The situation was reviewed by Sir Ian Hamilton as follows:—

"The country is broken, mountainous, and void of supplies. The water found in the areas occupied by our forces is quite inadequate for their needs, the only practicable beaches are small, cramped breaks in impracticable lines of cliffs; with the wind in certain quarters no sort of landing is possible. The wastage by bombardment and wreckage of lighters and small craft has led to crisis after crisis in our carrying capacity, whilst over every single beach plays fitfully throughout each day a devastating shell fire at medium ranges."

The arrival of German U-boats during May, with bases at Pola and Cattaro in the Adriatic, added to the difficulties of the campaign.

Two British battleships, the *Triumph*, 11,800 tons, and the *Majestic*, 14,900 tons, were sunk during the last week in May by U21.

The battleship *Goliath*, 12,950 tons, was torpedoed off Morto Bay on May 13th by a Turkish destroyer, which had steamed down the Straits under cover of darkness. From this time the Allied troops on shore had to rely less on the support of naval guns until the shallow draught monitors sent out from England could take the place of battleships.

Reinforcements and stores had to be brought out from Mudros to the various landing places in small craft.

Another point which might induce the War Council to consider that the Gallipoli campaign should be abandoned was the situation in Russia.

It was a further misfortune for these operations that a Russian army which had assembled at Odessa and was allocated for the Bosphorus, thus causing the Turks to keep a strong force near Constantinople, had been sent to Galicia, thus liberating Turkish troops for service at the Dardanelles.

The Allies in Gallipoli could expect no military assistance in future from Russia in the vicinity of Constantinople. By May 16th the Russian armies from the Carpathian passes were in front of von Mackensen's army.

Sir Ian Hamilton summed up the situation: "On May 22nd all transports had to be despatched to Mudros for safety. Thenceforth men, stores, guns, horses, etc., had to be brought from Mudros—a distance of forty miles—in fleet-

THE DARDANELLES CAMPAIGN 41

sweepers and other small and shallow craft less vulnerable to submarine attack. Every danger and difficulty was doubled."

However, in spite of these difficulties and the requirements of the Western Front, Sir Ian Hamilton was asked for an estimate of the troops he would need to gain his objective. The reply was that a further four divisions would be needed.

Only the 52nd Division could now be spared, and it was accordingly despatched. Further plans for offensive operations on a large scale could not for the present be made.

On the night of May 18th/19th a fresh division of the Turks vigorously attacked the Anzac front. At midnight heavy rifle and machine-gun fire burst out on most of the Turkish front, as well as bombing against the trenches, which were in close proximity.

At 0400 hours, the Turkish assaulting columns advanced against the right centre of the Anzac line. This assault was repulsed. By 0500 hours the Turks' attack in dense formations became general. It was everywhere repulsed, but it was pressed for the next five hours, in spite of heavy losses, estimated at 7,000. The Anzac losses were approximately 100 killed and 500 wounded. The security of the Anzac forward positions was now assured.

Round Quinn's Post the fighting was specially heavy on the night of May 20th/21st, and again the Turks were repulsed with heavy loss.

On May 24th an armistice had to be arranged for the burial of the Turkish dead.

Minor operations and raids then continued in this area till the end of July. The posts at the head of the Monash Gully were the centre of most of these actions. By this time our casualties were 38,636.

It was now realized that only by dispatching large reinforcements of men, munitions and war material could the Allies achieve their object.

The military situation on the Western Front prevented the full allotment of these requirements to this secondary theatre of war.

Trench warfare, therefore, had to be continued without the artillery support, which is almost indispensable for attacks against such strong positions which the Turks had now created.

Sir Ian Hamilton summed up the situation as follows:—

" The opposing fortified fronts stretched parallel from sea to straits. There was little space left now, either at Achi Baba or Gaba Tepe, for tactics which would fling flesh and blood battalions against lines of unbroken barbed wire. Advance must more and more tend to take the shape of concentrated attacks on small sections of the enemy's line after full artillery preparation. Siege warfare was soon bound to supersede manœuvre battles in the open. Consolidation and fortification of our front, improvement of approaches, selection of machine-gun emplacements, and scientific grouping of our artillery under a centralized control must ere long form the tactical basis of our plans."

The situation was not materially altered after the offensive operations of June 4th.

The result of these operations did, however, bring to notice the growing strength of the enemy, so that Lord Kitchener promised to send out three divisions of the new armies and the infantry of two Territorial Divisions. Unfortunately, a month was to pass before this promise could be fulfilled, as these troops were not to begin to arrive at Mudros until July 10th, and their concentrations would not be complete until August 10th.

On May 25th a raid was carried out by the navy, who landed troops at Nibrunesi Point. On this day there were minor engagements on the whole Helles front.

Preparations were being made for another general attack to be delivered on June 4th at Helles. The troops to take part in this attack, from right to left, were the 1st and 2nd French Divisions, 2nd Naval Brigade, 42nd Division, and 29th Division. The British front line—four thousand yards long—was held by 17,000 rifles, with 7,000 rifles in Corps Reserve, under General Hunter-Weston.

The advance began at midday on June 4th, after a first two and a half hours' bombardment, starting at 0800 hours, and another at 1130 hours, and continued until the moment of assault.

On the right of the line the 1st French Division was successful in capturing the trenches on their front. The 2nd French Division, on the left of the 1st Division, stormed and captured a strong redoubt at the head of Kereves Dere.

At this point of contact, however, between the French and British forces, the Turks were able to check the general advance. The Royal Naval Division obtained possession of the line of trenches immediately on their front.

On the left of this division, the Manchester Brigade of the 42nd Division, within half an hour, had advanced 500 yards into the Turkish second line. Further west, the 29th Division captured the Turks' front line trenches. On their left by the sea

THE DARDANELLES CAMPAIGN

the 29th Indian Brigade had heavy losses in trying to cross the enemy's barbed wire entanglements, which on their front had not been destroyed. Eventually, this brigade had to withdraw back to their own trenches.

The Turks in force now counter-attacked against the redoubt at the head of the Kereves Dere. They were well supported by artillery, and managed to re-take it. From this position they were able to enfilade the Royal Naval Division, who had to relinquish the redoubt which they had captured, and lost heavily in crossing open ground under machine-gun fire. In supporting this withdrawal the " Collingwood Battalion of the Royal Naval Division was practically destroyed." (Despatches.)

The Manchester Brigade, in the advanced position, which they gained, were, in their turn, enfiladed when the Royal Naval Division were back in their old trenches. This brigade suffered heavy losses during the five hours in which they maintained their position, in the hope that the rest of the line would come up to them again.

This advance, however, was not possible, and the Manchester Brigade had finally to withdraw to the first line of captured trenches. To maintain our positions the bulk of the troops in the reserve had been brought up to the forward positions.

The difficulty of maintaining positions had been that the advance was uneven, and could not be carried out simultaneously on the whole front owing to the enemy's superiority of artillery and the strength of their wire, which our artillery bombardment failed to damage sufficiently.

When one part of the line pushed ahead of the troops on their flanks they had heavy losses from enemy enfilade fire and from Turkish counter-attacks.

On the left of the French Corps' positions, the 2nd Division positions, immediate Turkish counter-attacks prevented any definite success from being obtained.

In the centre of the line there was a gain of ground up to four hundred yards.

It was not considered advisable to renew the attack on the following day in view of the increasing strength of the enemy's resistance and the superiority of their artillery. Information was also received as to the arrival of enemy reinforcements.

Orders were accordingly issued to consolidate the positions gained.

During the next ten days there were frequent Turkish attacks directed to regain the ground lost on June 4th.

On the night of June 11th/12th, on the front of the 29th Division, the Border Regiment and South Wales Borderers won two lines of trenches on their front.

On the night of June 16th/17th the Turks counter-attacked the positions gained on the 11th, and temporarily captured them. Our troops fell back to positions thirty yards in rear of them.

At dawn on June 12th the Dublin Fusiliers made a bayonet charge and regained the lost trenches.

On June 21st the French fought throughout the day for the capture of the Turkish positions on the eastern side of the Kereves Dere.

On the left of the French Corps' positions, the 2nd Division attacked and captured Haricot Redoubt and two lines of trenches by midday. On the right the 1st French Division were not at first successful in their attacks, so that the 2nd Division suffered in consequence from enfilade fire, as their right flank was exposed.

The 1st Division, however, struggled to improve their situation throughout the afternoon, and by 1830 hours had come into line with the 2nd Division and had captured six hundred yards of Turkish trenches above the Kereves Dere.

During this day the French lost 2,500, and the Turks, it was estimated, had lost 7,000 at least.

The attacks of the 1st Division were supported by all available British artillery, while the French battleship *St. Louis* bombarded the Turkish artillery on the Asiatic side of the Straits from the vicinity of Kum Kale.

Now that the right flank of the line at Helles had been advanced, it was decided to bring forward the left flank up the coast and towards Krithia. This operation was conducted by General Hunter-Weston on June 28th.

The troops at his disposal were the 29th Division, the 156th Brigade, and the 29th Indian Infantry Brigade.

The general plan was to pivot on a point in the front line a mile from the sea, and to advance the outer flank a thousand yards over five lines of Turkish trenches and over two lines of trenches on the inner flank.

In order to prevent the transfer of Turkish troops to Helles from Anzac an effective demonstration was carried out on the afternoon of June 28th.

Anzac troops advanced from Tasman Post on the right of their line above Brighton Beach to the lower spurs of Pine Ridge.

This movement had the desired effect, as the Turks brought troops up from Eski Keui to meet it. These reinforcements

THE DARDANELLES CAMPAIGN

were checked by artillery fire, and also by fire from destroyers. After dark the Anzac troops withdrew to their trenches.

The operation at Helles on June 28th started at 0900 hours with a bombardment of the nearest Turkish trenches by H.M.S. *Talbot*, while the field guns cut the enemy's wire.

At 1020 hours the bombardment increased in intensity. At 1045 hours the 1st Border Regiment rushed a small post called Boomerang Fort, built up on both sides of Saghir Dere, in front of the Turks' front line of trenches. At 1100 hours the artillery lengthened their range to cover the main advance.

East of the Saghir Dere the 4th and 7th Royal Scots captured two lines of Turkish trenches, but the remainder of the 156th Brigade on their right met with heavier opposition and were checked.

The 87th Brigade assaulted three lines of trenches between Saghir Dere and the sea, capturing three lines of trenches.

At 1130 hours the 86th Brigade passed through the 87th Brigade, and gained the final line of trenches up to the limit of the first allotted objectives.

The 29th Indian Brigade moved along the cliffs above the shore and captured the Knoll, situated on a spur running west of the furthest captured Turkish trench to the sea. The 1st Lancashire Fusiliers linked up this captured post with the left of the 86th Brigade.

On the right of the attacking line nearer Krithia a section of the enemy's trench lines were not captured. This section was attacked again at 1730 hours, but without success.

The British losses were 1,750 men, but the position had been definitely improved. Saghir Dere was in our possession, and our left flank now faced due east instead of north-east, and was within a mile from Krithia. Had there been ample reserves now available, it is probable that our objective in this area—Achi Baba—might have been secured.

"A whole mile along the coast, five lines of Turkish trenches, about two hundred prisoners, three mountain guns, and an immense quantity of small arms ammunition and many rifles" were captured during the operations on June 28th.

The Turkish counter-attacks on the two following nights were unsuccessful.

The last operation in June was a determined Turkish attack directed by Enver Pasha. His orders were to drive the Anzac Corps into the sea.

At midnight on the night of June 29th/30th heavy small arm and artillery fire was started, principally against that part of the line held by General Godley's Division.

At 0130 hours the Turks advanced with great determination

to assault the two fortified points, Pope's Hill and Quinn's Post, covering the eastern end of the Monash Gully. They were dispersed by the rifle and machine-gun fire of the 7th and 8th Light Horse Regiments by 0200 hours. Another attack an hour later against the left and left centre was similarly repulsed with heavy loss. Throughout June 30th the Turks attacked many points at both Helles and Anzac. Our naval guns and artillery broke up their concentrations by their fire near the Knoll, and also west of Krithia.

The losses incurred in this attack caused the Turks to realize the strength of the Anzac fortifications, as well as the determination with which they were held. The result was that the next month was quiet on the Anzac Front.

On our right flank at Helles the Turks attempted to make a surprise night attack on the night of June 29th/30th. Their movements were discovered by the searchlight of the *Wolverine* and checked.

At 0630 hours on June 30th the French Corps advanced their line and captured a fortified work called the Quadrilateral east of the source of the Kereves Dere.

The Turkish losses during the fighting at the end of June were estimated at 5,150 killed and 1,500 wounded. Our losses up to date had been approximately 42,000.

The whole problem of the operations in Gallipoli was now re-examined.

CHAPTER VIII.

July Plans and Preparations.

It was now clear that the Turkish positions were being made more formidable, and though we had been successful at a heavy cost in lives in improving our positions in the Kereves and Saghir ravines yet similar and stiffer obstacles would face our troops all the way up to the Bulair lines, which were fifty miles ahead.

Constantinople, strongly covered by fortications and by the Chatalja lines, lay 130 miles further on.

The Chatalja lines had their flanks resting on the Black Sea and on the Sea of Marmora. These lines were very strong and had never been forced.

The heat, the dust and the flies were causing sickness.

Local water supplies at Anzac had nearly given out during the dry season.

As a result of the casualties caused by disease and bombardment the divisions were very much below their strength, and no adequate provision was made for providing fresh drafts; also all the formations were supported by approximately only one third of their proportion of artillery.

During the first week in June the Allies were reinforced by the 52nd Division. Further reinforcements were due to begin to arrive on July 10th.

Three complete divisions and the infantry of two more Territorial divisions would bring the Allied Army up to a strength of thirteen divisions, four Anzac mounted brigades and one Indian brigade.

The final number of divisions in the Peninsula was as follows:—

Helles Corps.—29th Division, 42nd Division, 52nd Division, Royal Naval Division and two French Divisions.

Anzac Corps.—13th Division, Anzac Division, 1st Australian Division, 2nd Australian Division and 29th Indian Brigade.

Suvla Corps.—10th Division, 11th Division, 53rd Division, 54th Division, and 2nd Mounted Division (dismounted).

By the end of June, General Liman von Sanders had nine divisions under his command. He was aware, however, that additional troops were arriving for the Allies, and being uncertain as to their destination he felt obliged to leave troops on the Asiatic Coast of the Dardanelles, and also to keep a division in the vicinity of Gallipoli and one at Bulair.

The result of the deliberations by the War Council was that offensive operations were to be continued.

The additional five divisions were due to join by August 10th.

A fresh plan was, therefore, thought out for utilizing the services of the reinforcement against a fresh objective.

In the congested areas already occupied by our troops there was no scope for further operations without undue loss.

The general plan for the attack when the reinforcements had arrived was: first, to capture Sari Bair and then to gain " a position astride the Gallipoli Peninsula from the neighbourhood of Gaba Tepe to the straits north of Maidos." (Commander-in-Chief's order.) "Anzac was to deliver the knock-out blow; Helles and Suvla were complementary operations." (Despatches.)

For the most part July was a month of preparation for the main offensive operations to be undertaken in August, when reinforcements from England arrived.

Artillery ammunition too had to be carefully used.

The enemy were kept alert by a routine of bombing, sniping and mining in order to maintain the moral ascendancy of our troops and to make the Turks keep the same numbers at Helles.

The Turks at Krithia were reinforced early in July. At dawn on July 5th they made an attack from their front-line trenches. None of the attackers were able to reach either the French or British trenches, and few were able to get back to their own defences.

On July 12th and 13th operations similar to those undertaken on June 28th were carried out.

The French Corps attacked on the right flank and the 52nd Division on the right centre on a 3,000 yard front from the mouth of the Kereves Dere to the Sedd-el-Bahr—Krithia road.

The 29th Division, west of this road, and the Anzacs at Gaba Tepe were to contain the enemy on their front.

At 0735 hours on July 12th the Turks' trenches were attacked after a preliminary bombardment.

On the right flank the 1st Division of the French Corps gained ground beyond the Turks' second line, which the 2nd Division on their left had captured in co-operation with the 155th Brigade on their left. One battalion of the 155th Brigade, the 4th K.O.S.B., went past the Turks' third-line trenches until they were stopped by the enemy's cross-fire on their flanks. They were then forced to withdraw back to the second line of trenches held by the remainder of the Brigade.

The 157th Brigade on the left of the 155th Brigade captured

THE DARDANELLES CAMPAIGN

three lines of trenches approximately a hundred yards ahead of the Brigade on their right.

They maintained their position throughout the night in spite of the difficulty of dealing with counter-attacks on their exposed flanks.

On the following afternoon, July 13th, the attack was renewed at 1630 hours on the whole front.

The British were reinforced by a brigade of the Royal Naval Division. On both flanks the Allied line of attack was advanced so that new and valuable ground was gained.

The Turks' casualties were estimated at five thousand, and five hundred prisoners were taken.

The British lost three thousand casualties and advanced from two hundred to four hundred yards on different parts of the front.

The British casualties by the end of July numbered nearly fifty thousand.

When the expected reinforcements arrived there would be approximately a hundred and seven thousand rifles available.

By the end of July there were a hundred and ninety-four guns in the Peninsula, but the shortage of howitzers was still grave. In this hilly country these were specially required to support the advance of troops.

The Commander-in-Chief now considered the following courses:—

1. Landing every man on the southern sector of the Peninsula to advance to the Narrows.
2. Disembarking on the Asiatic side of the Dardanelles followed by a march on Chanak.
3. Landing at Enos to seize the neck of the isthmus at Bulair.
4. Reinforcing the Australian and New Zealand Corps combined with a landing in Suvla to capture the dominating heights of Sari Bair.

The last alternative was adopted.

The first course was rejected because (a) the space available was narrow and there was little free ground on which large bodies of troops could deploy; (b) even if Krithia was captured Achi Baba was too strongly held and entrenched to be assaulted without great loss; (c) Any landing-places would be under converging fire from Achi Baba and Kilid Bahr Plateau.

The second course was rejected because (a) the allied forces would be too weak to operate in two areas separated by the Dardanelles; (b) the attacks in the Peninsula would have to be continued and they would be in no greater strength than before.

The third course was not adopted because (*a*) there was an inadequate beach at the landing-place; (*b*) The fifty additional miles by sea to Enos would impose too great a strain on the fleet sweepers, trawlers and other vessels constantly engaged in carrying supplies; (*c*) the Turks had a strong army in Thrace; (*d*) even if the isthmus at Bulair was seized the Turks would be able to obtain supplies by ferrying them across the Sea of Marmora. The fourth plan was adopted, as it was hoped that by reinforcing the Anzacs it might be possible to make a strong enough advance to capture Sari Bair.

If a simultaneous fresh landing was made in Suvla Bay to surprise the Turks and make them dissipate their forces it might be possible for the Anzac Corps, after capturing Sari Bair, to seize Maidos and thus to cut off and isolate the Turks at Krithia and Achi Baba.

The tactical scheme was sound, and was the best of the four plans which had been considered.

The attack on Sari Bair had every possibility of succeeding and it only just fell short of achievement.

If the forces at Suvla had pushed on vigorously and gained their objectives, when they were lightly held, the Anzacs and their reinforcements might have maintained the positions which they had won.

Contributory reasons for the failure at Suvla have been put forward, namely, that there was lack of driving power among the commanders.

Sir Ian Hamilton's words on this subject were: "The one fatal error was inertia, and inertia prevailed."

That the troops landed at Suvla were untried, that there was lack of water ashore near the landing-places, and that there was defective staff work in some sectors have also been considered contributory causes.

A most important point, however, must be noted in the fact that the broken and diversified nature of the country made co-operation and inter-communication in the attack very difficult and gave every advantage to the Turks.

The details of the operations at Anzac were left to General Birdwood. He had available 37,000 rifles and 72 guns. Four monitors, two cruisers and two destroyers would support his attack.

General Stopford was in command of the troops at Suvla Bay co-operating with General Birdwood's force.

He had 30,000 rifles under his command of the 10th Division (less the 29th Brigade) and the 11th Division.

THE DARDANELLES CAMPAIGN

To contain the Turks at Helles there were 23,000 British and 17,000 French infantry.

The Turkish forces at Helles and Anzac were twelve divisions.

Throughout July the naval and military staffs worked out the landing arrangements for the troops.

A storage reservoir holding 30,000 gallons of water was secretly constructed at Anzac. A pack-mule corps of 4,650 mules was organized mainly for the distribution of water, and 1,750 water-carts were provided. A steamer was specially fitted with water-pumps, hose, tanks and troughs for use at Suvla. Water-lighters and a tank steamer to tow them were provided.

Under cover of darkness during the first week in August the 13th Division, 29th Infantry Brigade, and 29th Indian Infantry Brigade, namely, 25,000 men, with supplies, transport and eighty tons of water daily were landed at Anzac on the nights of August 3rd, 4th and 5th, and were concealed in prepared hiding places.

Devices were practised to mislead the enemy as to the main intentions of the operations.

Monitors took soundings and registered for their guns on points between Gaba Tepe and Kum Tepe.

Naval demonstrations were made at Mitylene where the 10th Division was assembled, and troops were landed there. A surprise landing by a small force was carried out at the northern side of the Gulf of Saros.

CHAPTER IX.

August: Offensive Operations at Anzac and Helles.

OPERATIONS started at Helles at 1600 hours on August 6th. This date was also settled for the attack from Anzac and the landing at Suvla. This date was fixed owing to the moon's late rising on August 7th.

The Commander-in-Chief moved his headquarters to Imbros. This island was the centre of the cable system. He could be at Helles, fifteen miles away, in fifty minutes; at Anzac, twelve miles away, in forty-five minutes; and at Suvla, nine miles away, in forty minutes. Mudros was sixty miles from Helles, sixty-five from Anzac, and seventy from Suvla.

Had he been at any one of his three areas of operations he would, he explained later, have lost his sense of proportion. He could, also, from his new headquarters best control the two divisions which he had in reserve.

An important factor for success was the rapidity with which the Allies could gain their objectives.

The Turks, owing to the secrecy with which the preparations for the attack had been made, were ignorant of the actual direction of the blow. They were, therefore, much dispersed.

General Liman von Sanders had organized his forces into two groups: one was watching at Helles, and one was at Anzac. He had two divisions in the north of the Peninsula and a large reserve at Chanak. He might not, therefore, be able to concentrate his forces and bring his reserves across the Narrows before Sari Bair was captured if all went well for the Allies at the outset.

The operations on August 6th started at 1600 hours at Helles. The VIII Corps attacked the Turkish trenches on their front and found them to be held in strength, as the Turks were standing to arms ready to make an attack with two new divisions that had recently arrived to relieve two others.

Our main attack was repulsed and the small gains on our left flank had to be relinquished after dark when the Turks counter-attacked in force.

The operations at Anzac began one and a half hours after the attacks were started by the VIII Corps at Helles. The general plan was for the troops to move along the shore in four columns after dark on August 6th, then wheel to the right and attack the Turks' position on Sari Bair from the north-west by night. Further attacks on the Anzac front were to be made from 400 Plateau to Nek.

THE DARDANELLES CAMPAIGN 53

The Anzac Corps when reinforced by the 13th Division from Helles and the 29th Brigade of the 10th Division was approximately 37,000 rifles and 72 guns.

To co-operate with the offensive operations at Anzac another surprise was to be given the Turks; namely, the 10th Division (less one brigade) and the 11th Division were to land at Suvla Bay on the night of August 6th/7th, and after securing a new base they were to join up with the left flank of General Birdwood's force.

The operations at Anzac started at 1730 hours with an assault delivered by the 1st Australian Brigade against the Turks' trenches on the 400 Plateau. After heavy fighting, this brigade was able to capture the trenches on their front and later to repulse the Turks' counter-attacks.

These operations were described in despatches as follows: "One weak Australian Brigade numbering at the outset but 2,000 rifles, and supported only by two weak battalions, carried the work under the eyes of a whole enemy division, and maintained their grip upon it like a vice during six days' successive counter-attacks."

Turkish reserves who might have been fighting on the Turks' right flank or at Suvla Bay were contained by the assaults of the 2nd Australian Brigade and a Light Horse regiment on Baby Trench, Hill 700, and German Officer's Trench, respectively one mile and six hundred yards north of Lone Pine, and also on Battleship Hill two hundred yards north-east of Baby Trench, although no ground was gained at these places.

The forces at Anzac were divided into two parts. One part, consisting of the Australian and New Zealand Division (less the 1st and 3rd Light Horse Brigades), the 13th Division (less five battalions), the 29th Indian Infantry Brigade, and an Indian Mountain Artillery Brigade, was to attack the Sari Bair Heights. The other part, consisting of the Australian Division, the 1st and 3rd Light Horse Brigades, and two batteries of the 40th Brigade, was to contain the Turks on their front and to make special attacks on the Turkish positions.

The details of the plan for the capture of Sari Bair were as follows:—

The force detailed for this operation was to advance in four columns on the night of August 6th/7th towards the summits of Sari Bair from the northern end of Anzac on the shore near No. 2 Outpost at Fisherman's Hut.

On reaching their assembly positions they were to wheel to the east and work up the water-courses Sazli Beit, Chailak and Aghyl, leading to the highest ridges of Sari Bair.

The four columns carrying out the attack were divided up as follows:—

Right covering column, in which were the New Zealand Mounted Rifles Brigade and Otago Mounted Rifles Regiment.

Right assaulting column, in which were the New Zealand Infantry Brigade and Indian Mountain Battery (less one section).

Left covering column, in which were the Headquarters of the 40th Brigade and two battalions.

Left assaulting column, in which were the 29th Indian Infantry Brigade, 4th Australian Infantry Brigade, and Indian Mountain Battery (less one section).

The Divisional Reserve consisted of two battalions at Chailak Dere and the 39th Infantry Brigade, and a half a Field Company, R.E., at Aghyl Dere.

The right assaulting column was to advance up Suzli Beit Dere and Chailak Dere ravines and to capture Chunuk Bair.

The left assaulting column was to advance up the Aghyl Dere ravine and capture Koja Chemen Tepe.

The covering columns were to clear the ravines and foothills and to let the assaulting columns go through to capture the final objectives.

The Commander-in-Chief described the preliminary operations as follows:—

One of the assaulting columns was " to capture the enemy's positions commanding the foothills, first to open the mouths of the ravines, secondly to cover the right flank of another covering force while it marched along the beach. The other covering column was to strike far out to the north until, from a hill called Damakjelik Bair, it could at the same time facilitate the landing of the IX Corps at Nibrunesi Point, and guard the left flank of the column assaulting Sari Bair from any forces of the enemy which might be assembled in the Anafarta Valley."

At the outset of this operation the Turkish posts on the lower spurs were surprised and captured. The enemy's detachments were driven back at all points in the gullies, so that soon after midnight the outlets were in possession of the covering columns.

Then the tracks by which the advance had to be continued were most difficult to find in the dark. The country was unknown and more intricate than had been anticipated.

Progress was slower during the night than had been expected with the result that at dawn the leading troops were

THE DARDANELLES CAMPAIGN   55

still some distance from their objectives on Chunuk Bair and Hill 305 at dawn.

The troops also were very much exhausted by their exertions in climbing the rocky sides of the hills and in breaking through the scrub.

The details of the operations during this important night, August 6th/7th, were as follows:—

The right covering column had as its final objective the capture of Chailak Dere and Sazli Beit Dere ravines. First it was necessary to seize the redoubt named No. 3 Post. This post was captured without difficulty, as the Turks were completely surprised. The surprise was obtained by regularly shelling No. 3 Post at 2100 hours from H.M.S. *Colne* for half an hour. Then nothing happened. On the night of August 6th/7th the usual routine was carried out and, as before, the Turks vacated their fort until they thought that all would be quiet again.

On this night the Auckland Mounted Rifles were waiting in the vicinity, and were able to rush the redoubt without opposition. When the Turks tried to recapture it they were easily driven off.

The New Zealanders then quickly advanced and cleared Bauchop's Hill. They were then successful in storming and capturing Table Top, a hill 400 feet high with nearly precipitous sides, by midnight. One hundred and fifty prisoners and much ammunition were captured.

While the right covering column was advancing, the left covering column proceeded up the Aghyl Dere. Strong opposition was encountered at Damakjelik Bair, which was finally rushed by the South Wales Borderers.

By 0130 hours the right assaulting column had passed through their covering column in Sazli Beit Dere and were attacking Rhododendron Spur. Owing to the difficulty of the country and the considerable opposition encountered, this spur was not captured before 0530 hours. Here their position was consolidated, but it was still a quarter of a mile from their final objective on Chunuk Bair.

The left assaulting column, after crossing Chailak Dere, entered Aghyl Dere. Here the two brigades of this column separated up the two forks of the ravine. The 4th Australian Brigade went up the northern fork, and the 29th Indian Brigade went up the southern fork.

The Australians were able to reach the northern end of Azmak Dere. The Indian Brigade was able to capture the ridge west of the farm below Chunuk Bair on the lower slopes of Hill Q by 0700 hours on August 7th and were able to get into touch with the New Zealanders on Rhododendron Spur and also with the Australians.

As it had not been possible for the attack to be launched against the troops on the summit of the main ridge of Chunuk Bair until 0930 hours on August 7th, all hope of surprising the enemy had gone.

By midday the enemy were still in possession of the main ridge, and their reinforcements were being brought up. It was necessary, therefore, to discontinue further attacks and to reorganize the forces for a fresh attack on the following day.

The forces were now rearranged into right, centre, and left columns.

The right column was the right assaulting column with the Auckland Mounted Rifles added to it, and also two battalions of the 13th Division and the Maori Contingent.

The centre and left columns under General Cox contained the 21st Indian Mountain Battery (less one section), 4th Australian Brigade, 39th Infantry Brigade (less one battalion), 29th Indian Brigade, and the 6th Bn. The South Lancashire Regiment.

The orders for the attack on August 8th were for the right column to attack and capture the summit of Chunuk Bair and for the left column to capture Hill 305.

The Turkish detachments on these objectives had by this time been reinforced by a division, and they were ready to meet the assaults.

The operations of the right column started at 0415 hours. The New Zealand Infantry Brigade led the advance, and after a most determined assault secured a footing on Chunuk Bair. In spite of very heavy cross-fire, they held this position throughout the day unsupported by the other columns.

The central column, operating from the southern fork of the Aghyl Dere, could make little progress owing to the strength of the opposition, while the left column had difficulty in maintaining their position in the Azmak Dere.

The Commander-in-Chief described the situation as follows: " Here they stood at bay and, though the men were by now half-dead with thirst and fatigue, they bloodily repulsed attack after attack delivered by heavy columns of Turks."

Substantial support had been expected from the troops landing at Suvla. Actually this assistance did not materialize beyond drawing from the Anzac troops the attention of the Turkish troops, which General Liman von Sanders had moved from the vicinity of Gallipoli as soon as he realized where our main offensive operations were being carried out. It was unfortunate that the troops at Suvla, by not occupying the

THE DARDANELLES CAMPAIGN 57

Anafarta Ridges, could not join up with the left flank of the Anzac Corps on August 8th.

It was decided to continue the offensive operations on the following day, and to work forward from the position already gained on the summit of Chunuk Bair.

The force was now divided into three columns:

No. 1 column was to consolidate and improve the positions already gained on the right.

No. 2 column was directed to advance up the valley between Chunuk Bair and Hill Q, and to co-operate with No. 3 column in the attack on this hill.

No. 3 column was to concentrate behind No. 1 column, then to clear the summit of Chunuk Bair, then cross the valley leading to Hill Q after it had been cleared by No. 2 column, and to deliver the main attack on Hill Q.

The day's operations started with a heavy bombardment of Chunuk Bair and Hill Q at dawn on August 9th.

No. 1 column maintained their position as ordered in spite of strong Turkish counter-attacks.

No. 2 column carried out its allotted task. The troops in this column, however, were unsupported at the moment when they were expecting the co-operation of No. 3 column for the assault on Hill Q.

By the time that No. 2 column had cleared the valley between Hill Q and Chunuk Bair, No. 3 column should have cleared this latter hill, so that both columns could have gone forward together in the attack.

No. 3 column had lost direction in the very difficult ground in Chailak Dere leading up to their assembly position behind No. 1 column. At the time when it should have been on Chunuk Bair it was debouching at the Farm.

The Turkish commander on Hill Q now counter-attacked the isolated No. 2 column, and drove them back to their starting-point.

The commander of No. 3 column, on finding that he was too late to assist in the capture of Hill Q, formed up to attack the northern summit of Chunuk Bair. Two battalions reached this objective at the time when No. 3 column had fallen back. Withdrawal was then carried out back to the Farm.

Throughout the rest of the day the fighting centred round No. 1 column, whose troops continued to hold the position they had won on Chunuk Bair, but were unable to retain their position on the crest of this hill.

The Turks, however, were in force, as they had been reinforced by their 8th Division. They had the advantage in their position of better observation and field of fire than the Anzac troops had. Nor did the Turks suffer from want of water, and there were not the same difficulties in the supply situation as there were for the Anzacs.

During the night No. 1 column was relieved by the 6th Bn. The Loyal North Lancashires and the 5th Bn. The Wiltshire Regiment. The 10th Bn. The Hampshire Regiment were to continue the line to the Farm. These troops were heavily shelled at dawn on August 10th before they had properly settled down in their trenches.

The troops on Chunuk Bair were then attacked by the 8th Turkish Division and three additional battalions. Our troops were driven off the crest of the hill and beyond the Farm. When the Turks followed up their successes down the western side of the summit they were met by our heavy fire from naval and land guns.

By 1000 hours, after desperate hand-to-hand fighting, the Turkish attack was checked. The Turks, however, held the top of Chunuk Bair and had regained much ground which had been gained early on August 7th. The total casualties of the Anzacs had now reached 12,000.

As Sir Ian Hamilton wrote: " The grand coup had not come off. The Narrows were still out of sight and beyond field-gun range."

The Anzacs' position had, however, been considerably extended in a northerly direction. Damakjelik Bair and the high ground between the Sazli Beit and Chailak Dere had been gained. This gave the Anzac troops more space for manœuvre and made it possible to effect a junction on August 12th with the troops landed at Suvla.

CHAPTER X.

Operations at Suvla Bay.

The landing at Suvla Bay was started at 2230 hours on August 6th, half an hour after the operations at Anzac began.

These operations were conducted by General Stopford, commanding the IX Corps (less the 13th Division and the 29th Brigade).

As far as was known at the time the Turks had some defences on Hill 10, on the ridge beyond Suvla Point and round Lala Baba, a knoll between Salt Lake and Nibrunesi Point. They had also fortifications and some guns on Chocolate Hill, and Ismail Oglu Tepe. Their total strength was approximately 4,000 in the area where the landing was taking place.

The general plan was that the first landing should be made by the 11th Division at Beaches " A," " B " and " C " before dawn on August 7th.

They were to leave Imbros in destroyers and motor-lighters after dark on August 6th, so that the disembarkation could begin during the hours of darkness before midnight.

The 11th Division was then to capture Ismail Oglu Tepe, Chocolate Hill and Kiretch Tepe Sirt by daybreak.

The remainder of the Army Corps were then to occupy the Anafarta Hills, and to join up with the Anzac Corps.

It was hoped then to drive the Turks off Sari Bair and to hold a line across the Peninsula from Gaba Tepe to Maidos.

The 32nd and 33rd Brigades landed at " C " Beach, south of Nibrunesi Point. The 34th Brigade landed at " A " Beach in Suvla Bay, just east of Suvla Point. The landings were made at the allotted times.

By 0200 hours two battalions of the 32nd Brigade attacked and captured Lala Baba. The Turks in this area retired to Hill 10.

At " A " Beach the Turks were alert. It was most unfortunate that at this beach the lighters grounded before land was reached, and the troops had to struggle through nearly five feet of water under cross-fire from Turkish outposts on Lala Baba and Ghazi Baba. This caused some delay.

Soon after dawn the 34th Brigade, supported by the 32nd Brigade, attacked Hill 10.

One battalion, the 11th Manchester Regiment, proceeded beyond Hill 10 up the Karakol Dagh, where they encountered and drove back the few Turkish troops on outpost duty there.

THE DARDANELLES CAMPAIGN

The advance in this area was not as satisfactory as had been hoped, as there was some confusion between the units of the 32nd and 34th Brigades.

"No one," Sir Ian Hamilton wrote, "seems to have been present, who could take hold of the two brigades and launch them in a concerted and cohesive attack. Consequently there was confusion and hesitation, increased by gorse fires lit by hostile shells."

Hill 10 was eventually captured by two battalions of the 34th Brigade.

The Turks retreated slowly towards Sulajik and Kuchuk Anafarta Ova, followed up the 32nd and 34th Brigades.

At this time, soon after dawn on August 7th, the 31st Brigade and two battalions of the 30th Brigade arrived near Nibrunesi Point and were anchored there.

They were disembarked at "C" Beach and were ordered to support the left flank of the 11th Division at Hill 10.

As they were disembarked at "C" Beach instead of "A" Beach, they had to march an extra four miles before they came into action near Hill 10.

Soon after 0800 hours more battalions of the 10th Division from Mudros Bay arrived and were disembarked close to Beach "A."

Later three more battalions of the 10th Division were landed near Ghazi Baba. The G.O.C. 10th Division at once sent troops to operate towards Karakol Dagh. A footing was gained on its western edge.

Orders were then changed and the available battalions of the 10th Division were ordered to operate on the right flank of the 11th Division and to capture Chocolate Hill and Green Hill, while the 34th and 32nd Brigades advanced against Kuchuk Anafarta.

Thus the reserve of the 10th Division had to march back and round Salt Lake, and valuable time was lost when it was vitally important to capture the heights dominating Suvla Plain before the Turks could occupy them in force and consolidate their position there.

The 33rd Brigade captured Chocolate Hill early in the afternoon with the loss of only a few casualties.

This Brigade was unable to capture its second objective, Ismail Oglu Tepe, owing to increasing Turkish opposition.

Thus, the troops by the afternoon of August 7th were a long way from their objectives on Biyuk Anafarta.

Lala Baba, Ghazi Baba, Chocolate Hill, Ismail Oglu Tepe and Kiretch Tepe should have been in possession of the 11th Division by daybreak.

THE DARDANELLES CAMPAIGN

The troops landing later were to advance into line with the Anzacs struggling to capture Sari Bair.
The difficulties of this operation were considerable.
The 11th Division, who had had no previous war experience, were directed to capture six widely separated positions in an unknown, unreconnoitred country, under cover of darkness, without guides and against opposition.
By the evening of August 7th Chocolate Hill, Green Hill and Sulajik had been captured and a position had been gained on the southern end of Karakol Dagh.
The Turks made no attempt to counter-attack during the night, as their forces in this area were too weak for any offensive operations.
On the following day, August 8th, the IX Corps at Suvla had a great opportunity to capture the original objectives assigned to them, while the enemy in their front were still weak and disorganized.
Unfortunately, little action was taken at this important time. The troops had for the most part practically a day of rest and reorganization.
The only forward movements were the occupation of Scimitar Hill by two battalions of the 32nd Brigade and another battalion occupied ground up to Abrikja. The 10th Division advanced their positions on Kiretch Tepe Sirt.
Sir Ian Hamilton described the position as follows: " Divisional Commanders believed themselves to be unable to move. Their objections overbore the Corps Commander's resolution. Thus a priceless twelve hours had already gone to help the chances of the Turkish reinforcements, which were, I knew, both from naval and aerial sources, actually on the march for Suvla."
The main reasons urged for not advancing on August 8th were (*a*) disorganization and fatigue after a night landing, followed by fights against an enemy dispersed over a wide area in an unknown country; (*b*) want of water, as the distribution from the beaches was not yet working efficiently; (*c*) inadequate artillery support.
Sir Ian Hamilton wrote in this connection: " Driving power was required, and even a certain ruthlessness to brush aside pleas for a respite for tired troops. The one fatal error was inertia. And inertia prevailed."
In view of the great local numerical superiority of the IX Corps on August 8th, there can be no doubt Sir Ian Hamilton's stricture was justified.
It is also true that there was weakness in artillery support, as only one field battery and two mountain batteries were

ashore; and, in addition, the difficulties of intercommunication made effective naval support difficult.

Sir Ian Hamilton writes in his despatches with reference to artillery support the following: "Normally it may be correct to say that in modern warfare infantry cannot be expected to advance without artillery preparation. But in a landing on a hostile shore the order is inverted. The infantry must advance and seize a position suitable to cover the landing and to provide artillery positions for the main thrust. The very existence of the force, its water supply, its facilities for munitions and supplies, and its power to reinforce, must depend upon the infantry being able instantly to make good sufficient ground without aid of artillery other than can be supplied for the purpose by floating batteries."

The situation on August 8th was evidently one demanding resolute and immediate action.

The Commander-in-Chief at his headquarters at Imbros made a personal intervention in the evening when he realized the state of inaction that prevailed at Suvla.

Aeroplane reconnaissance had revealed that during the day the Turks were removing their guns, and that hostile reinforcements were being brought up from Bulair.

Therefore there was a great opportunity for the attackers on August 8th to carry out the first part of their programme and capture the heights east of their landing-place, while there were still only Turkish detachments in front of the two British divisions.

The inevitable Turkish counter-attack could not take place during that day.

It could not, however, be known then to the IX Corps Commander that this was the case. He could not tell that General Liman von Sanders at Gallipoli only had the first intimation on the night of August 6th-7th that the Allies were landing at Suvla, and that there were also heavy attacks against the Turkish positions at Sari Bair.

When von Sanders did realize the whole situation he sent the two divisions at his disposal towards Suvla.

To reach their destination would mean at least two days' marching for them on the poor roads available.

The IX Corps Commander could, however, realize, that there was little opposition to any advance, and that it was vitally important to capture the hills overlooking his present positions before the enemy occupied them in force.

When the Commander-in-Chief visited Suvla on the evening of August 8th he found that everything was peaceful there, and realizing that a day had been lost urged that an immediate attack should be made on the Anafarta Hills.

THE DARDANELLES CAMPAIGN 63

The Corps Commander then reported that the 11th Divisional Commander disliked the idea of an advance by night, and that he did not care to insist on such an operation being carried out, although personally he was eager to advance.

Sir Ian Hamilton then interviewed the commander of the 11th Division, who saw the danger of not occupying the high ground dominating the Suvla Plain.

The G.O.C. 11th Division, however, declared that it was impossible at 1800 hours to arrange for a night attack with his troops scattered over the country as they were.

Eventually it was discovered that the 32nd Brigade was more concentrated than the others and therefore could carry out offensive operations and endeavour to anticipate the Turkish reinforcements on the tactical points of the Anafarta Hills.

Sir Ian Hamilton therefore directed that this brigade should advance at the earliest possible moment.

Actually this brigade was not concentrated, as two of its battalions were on Hill 70, and on a spur called Abrikja, northeast of it.

In order to concentrate the Brigade these two battalions were withdrawn from their advantageous positions for the general brigade attack to be started at 0400 hours on August 9th.

When the advance did start the opposition encountered was not serious at first.

The 11th Division reached the Turkish positions on Kuchuk Anafarta at 0530 hours.

A company of the East Yorks attached to the 32nd Brigade succeeded in occupying a position on Tekke Tepe, commanding the whole of the Anafarta Sagir.

On the right of the 32nd Brigade, the 31st Brigade gained a footing on Scimitar Hill, but could not maintain their position there.

Further south, on the right of the 11th Division, the 33rd Brigade attacked soon after 0500 hours on August 9th and gained a position on Ismail Oglu Tepe. The Turkish 12th Division were now in the field opposed to the 11th Division and were able to recover Ismail Oglu Tepe and Scimitar Hill after strong counter-attacks.

The 32nd Brigade fell back on to Sulajik again. The 33rd Brigade thereupon abandoned Ismail Oglu Tepe and withdrew to Chocolate Hill, assisted by two battalions of the 34th Brigade.

The Commander-in-Chief ordered up two battalions of the

53rd Division, which had arrived at Suvla Bay during the night of August 8th-9th.

This reserve advancing on the left flank rendered useful assistance until ammunition supply became difficult.

The result of the day's fighting was that the 11th Division withdrew back to its original position after having suffered heavy losses.

The Turks now made the high ground overlooking the Suvla Plain into a strong defensible position.

On the following day the Commander-in-Chief decided to attack the Anafarta positions again.

This time the 53rd Division were to carry out the attack, supported by the 11th Division and 59th Field Brigade R.A., two Highland mountain batteries and the guns of warships.

The Turks were fully prepared and had been reinforced since the previous day, and also had consolidated their position.

The 53rd Division gained some ground at the outset, but was finally obliged to fall back to a general line running from the Azmak Dere through Green Hill and west of Kuchuk Anafarta Ova to the position held by the 10th Division on the Kiretch Tepe Sirt.

Further frontal attacks, it was now considered, would be useless, so the IX Corps Commander ordered the line now occupied to be entrenched and held.

The IX Corps had, therefore, not been able fully to carry out their allotted rôle of helping the Anzac troops or of containing the Turkish reinforcements sent from Bulair. The 12th Turkish Division only was engaged at Suvla, the 7th Turkish Division went direct to the Sari Bair area.

On August 12th Sir Ian Hamilton directed that the 54th Division should make a night march and dawn attack on August 13th on the Turkish positions at Kavak Tepe and Tekke Tepe, the crowning heights of the Anafarta Hills.

The IX Corps Commander considered that it would be a better plan first to clear the close and intricate ground north of Sulajik at Kuchuk Anafarta Ova in order that the night march might be undertaken without interference from the enemy.

Accordingly the 163rd Brigade were ordered to carry out this operation. The enemy were found to be in force. The result was that there was considerable fighting in this area.

The night march and attack were abandoned.

The Corps Commander considered that even if the attack succeeded he would find it difficult to supply the troops in positions gained in the hills. The project had, therefore, been dropped.

THE DARDANELLES CAMPAIGN 65

It was hoped to renew the assaults on Sari Bair on August 13th, while the 11th and 54th Divisions attacked Ismail Oglu Tepe.

This scheme had to be abandoned because on further investigation it was found that the Anzac troops were unable to carry out this attack.

On August 15th an attack was carried out on the left flank with the object of bringing this flank in line with the centre of the position and of gaining possession of the whole of the Kiretch Tepe Sirt ridge. The 30th and 31st Brigades of the 10th Division attacked along the top of the ridge, supported on the right in the low ground by the 162nd Brigade of the 54th Division.

Our ships, *Grampus* and *Foxhound*, bombarded the Turkish right from the Gulf of Saros.

At first, considerable progress was made on the northern slope of the ridge facing the sea in spite of the difficulties of the country and of the stout defence on the part of the Turks.

On the southern side of the ridge the advance was quickly checked, owing to the heavy fire of the Turkish artillery and to the fact that the defenders were not surprised and had reinforcements ready on the spot.

The result of the day's fighting was that the left flank of the 10th Division was considerably advanced.

During the night and on August 16th the Turks counter-attacked, and being well supplied with grenades, of which our troops were then deficient, were able to drive back with heavy loss the battalions which had advanced on the previous day.

In this intersected country the hand grenade would have been specially valuable, and the want of this weapon in sufficient quantities was mainly the cause of our heavy losses and withdrawal.

Finally the 10th Division were forced back to their original line; and in the Suvla Bay area the troops soon settled down to trench warfare after contact had been obtained with the troops at Anzac.

It was now estimated that there were 20,000 Turks opposing our troops at Suvla.

During the third week in August further reinforcements were, for the time being, refused, and so the fate of the Dardanelles enterprise was practically settled.

On August 15th General de Lisle assumed temporary command of the IX Corps.

F

On August 16th the line held by the IX Corps in the Suvla Bay area ran from the Azmak Dere through Hetman Chair, Green Hill, Sulajik and Kuchuk Anafarta Ova over Kiretch Tepe Sirt to the sea.

In this area were the 10th Division (less one brigade), the 11th, 53rd, and 54th Divisions, totalling approximately 30,000 rifles.

CHAPTER XI

OPERATIONS AND PLANS LEADING TO THE EVACUATION.

AFTER the deadlock at Suvla there was some indecision as to the future operations at Gallipoli. The effect upon the public morale of evacuation was feared, and so was the loss to be incurred during the actual operation, as well as the heavy casualty list, which would certainly occur if a further advance in force was attempted.

The Turks at Anzac and Suvla, including local reserves, had, it was considered, 75,000 rifles. In addition, in reserve they had 45,000 rifles twenty miles north of the Gulf of Saros. They could replace casualties within twenty-four hours from their capital, 150 miles away, whereas it would take a month for reinforcements to reach the front line at Gallipoli from England, 3,000 miles away by sea. The Australians' home reinforcements were seven thousand miles away, and the New Zealanders ten thousand miles away.

The Commander-in-Chief telegraphed to the War Office to ask for 45,000 men to replace casualties, and a further 50,000 in addition.

The British Government, however, were not disposed to send any more troops to Gallipoli at this time.

Three alternate rôles, therefore, had to be considered for the troops in Gallipoli, disposed, as they were, in a most unfavourable situation, with their positions overlooked and under shell fire up to and including the landing places, which also were at the mercy of the wind.

The Turks were receiving reinforcements to replace casualties and ammunition. Our nearest large reserves of ammunition were at Marseilles, 1,400 miles overseas.

The force at Gallipoli, unless reinforced, was too small to gain the original objectives. The positions on the fringe of the Peninsula could, therefore, either be held or evacuated.

The Commander-in-Chief, in order to hold the position more advantageously at Suvla, decided to improve it by an advance towards the Anafarta Heights.

He decided to move the 29th Division by night in trawlers from Cape Helles to Suvla, and to bring the 2nd Mounted Division from Egypt to Suvla.

By August 21st there were five divisions under General de Lisle.

The first objective for the attack on this day was to be the capture of Ismail Oglu Tepe before seizing the Anafarta Hills.

The 53rd and 54th Divisions were to contain the enemy on their front between Sulajik and Kiretch Tepe Sirt.

The 29th and 11th Divisions were to advance respectively from Chocolate Hill and from Azmak Dere.

The 29th Division was to assault Scimitar Hill as a first objective, and later to attack Ismail Oglu Tepe.

The 11th Division was to clear the Turks out of their positions at Aire Kavak and Hetman Chair, and later to co-operate from the south-west, with the 29th Division in the attack on Ismail Oglu Tepe.

The 10th and 2nd Mounted Divisions were in Corps Reserve.

The Anzac Corps were to advance on the left of their line from Damakjelik Bair to the line Kabak Kuyu and Susak Kuyu.

The preliminary bombardment was timed to start at 1430 hours on August 21st. The infantry were to advance half-an-hour later. It was hoped that at this time the sun would be in the eyes of the Turks, and that their trenches would be clearly shown up to the attackers. Unfortunately a mist enveloped the Suvla Bay area, concealing the enemy's position. Artillery support was, therefore, very difficult for the attackers.

The Turks were not surprised by our attack. They were strongly entrenched, and were supported by forty-eight guns and eight five-inch howitzers. They had observation over all the ground over which an advance would have to be made to their position.

Our bombardment started as ordered—at 1430 hours—against the enemy's positions; for the most part on Ismail Oglu Tepe and Scimitar Hill.

The advance of the leading brigades of the 11th Division started at 1500 hours, in accordance with the plans.

The 34th Brigade on the right was successful in capturing its first objective, namely, the Turkish trenches between Aire Kavak and Hetman Chair.

The 32nd Brigade, on the left of the 34th Brigade, was to capture Hetman Chair. This Brigade took a wrong direction, advancing on the final objective, Ismail Oglu Tepe, in a north-east direction instead of due east. While they were correcting their line of advance they were attacked and checked by the Turks.

The 33rd Brigade was hurried up from the Divisional Reserve, and similarly lost direction. Part reinforced the 32nd Brigade and part went in a southerly direction towards Susak Kuyu.

When the 29th Division attacked, one battalion gained a footing on Scimitar Hall, but was shelled off it later and had to withdraw.

THE DARDANELLES CAMPAIGN

Part of the 29th Division advanced beyond Green Hill, but as the Division on their right was then behind their flank all attempts to push further forward became impracticable.

The 2nd Mounted Division advanced across the open plain for Lala Baba via Chocolate Hill. They advanced an appreciable distance, in spite of heavy losses from Turkish resistance and shell fire. Eventually they had to fall back with the rest of the force to the positions originally held.

On the Anzac side, General Cox's force, consisting of the 29th Indian Brigade, New Zealand Mounted Rifles, and units from the 10th and 13th Divisions, advanced towards Hill 60, beyond Damakjelik Bair. A well at Kabak Kuju was obtained. This was a great acquisition in this waterless area.

The positions gained made it possible during the next few days to join the left of the Anzac front to the right of the Suvla front, on the northern side of Azmak Dere.

The Turkish positions were too well entrenched and too well placed for any purely frontal offensive operations over the open to be successfully carried out, except on a very large scale, with more artillery support than could be expected to be available.

Only near Hill 60 had there been any advance. The losses of the 29th Division alone had been approximately 5,000. It was unlucky that the mist prevented an effective bombardment, but it is doubtful if any impression could have been made with the available forces, in view of the strength of the enemy's dominating positions.

The forces at Anzac were now strengthened by the arrival of 2nd Australian Division, composed of two infantry brigades.

On August 27th a composite force, under General Cox, began operations, which, by August 29th, enabled them to gain possession of Hill 60. A continuous line of twelve miles of trenches was now linked up from close to Gaba Tepe to the Gulf of Saros at the foot of Kiretch Tepe Sirt. The beaches were exposed to artillery fire. Unfortunately this line was overlooked for the most part by the enemy on the Anafarta Hills and at Sari Bair.

The Allies now had to be content to carry out the passive rôle of trench warfare in positions which the August offensive had left them at a cost of 40,000 men.

The lack of success of the final offensive was no doubt due to the lack of support given to the left flank of the Anzac columns on August 7th and 8th, when they were fighting hard for the possession of Chunuk Bair. The Anzacs on these days were faced with growing hostile opposition.

By August 10th the Turks were too strong, and the Anzacs could not retain their gains on Chunuk Bair.

The situation after the final offensive at the beginning of September was not satisfactory from the point of view of the Allies.

The French Government was beginning to doubt the wisdom of continuing operations in Gallipoli.

The Allies' losses were not replaced. Reinforcements could not be expected until after the situation in Salonika had been stabilized, and until after the big offensive on the Flanders front had been completed.

The Turks were superior in numbers of rifles and in artillery, and had all the advantage of position from the point of view of fire and observation. Their positions, naturally strong, had been artifically strengthened. The available artillery at the disposal of the Allies would not be sufficient to render them temporarily untenable.

Communication with the navy would become more difficult as the autumn advanced.

The health of the troops was suffering, and consequently their fighting power would be diminished in the enervating Mediterranean climate. The dust, the flies, and the dreary surroundings were all lowering to the troops' vitality.

The Dardanelles Committee had now a difficult decision to make. A successor in this area was desired, but no new divisions could be spared for operations.

Only drafts amounting to approximately 13,000 and 12,000 second-line Territorials and dismounted Yeomanry were sent out, leaving the existing formations 30,000 below strength.

Fortunately, Marshal Liman von Sanders at this time adopted an unenterprising policy of passive defence. He realized that he was containing large forces, and that this campaign was proving a great drain on the fighting resources of the Allies.

On September 25th the Commander-in-Chief was informed that two British divisions and probably one French division must be taken for service at Salonika.

On October 11th the Commander-in-Chief was asked for his views as to the losses that would be incurred in evacuating the Peninsula.

This opinion was asked for in view of the strength of the enemy's position, the unsatisfactory state of health of the troops, the possible bad weather in the autumn and winter adding to the difficulties of inter-communication between ships and the shore, and even making the present position of the force untenable, and that large reserves of men and ammunition

THE DARDANELLES CAMPAIGN 71

required for further offensive operations were not forthcoming. In addition, the damage done to our shipping had been considerable.

During the campaign two battleships, twelve gunboats and minelayers, two hundred transports and supply ships had been sunk. Also the 1st French and 10th British Divisions had now been sent as an advanced force to Salonika.

On the other hand, there was the question of loss of prestige in the East to be considered. The answer sent to the suggested evacuation was that it was unthinkable and wrong, both politically and strategically.

The difficulty, however, for those responsible for our war policy was to provide sufficient men, guns and munitions for a third area of operations—Salonika—in which the offensive was to be undertaken.

A decision had to be arrived at as to whether to continue to attack the Germans on the Western Front or to continue to strike at weaker points in Gallipoli or in Salonika.

In France, the channel ports had to be defended, and our Russian Allies had to be helped in the Dardanelles. Our successes here might still have saved Russia from destruction and revolution, and gained the support of Bulgaria and Greece.

The Turks, if defeated, would not have been able to interfere with our interests at the head of the Persian Gulf or with the traffic on the Suez Canal.

While these points were being considered the winter weather was setting in.

The Dardanelles Committee was still being influenced in three different directions.

The rival claims of Gallipoli and Salonika had to be considered as a subsidiary theatre of operations, especially as it was now learnt that extra supplies of ammunition from Germany would shortly be reaching the Turks.

On October 16th, General Sir Ian Hamilton received orders to return to England.

On October 28th, General Sir Charles Monro arrived at Imbros to command the forces.

In November the Serbian Army was retreating towards the Adriatic.

The Allies at Salonika were occupying a zone to cover their landing places. The campaign in Gallipoli was languishing. Minor operations only were undertaken, such as the attack on November 15th by the 156th Brigade towards Krithia. This led to the capture of three hundred yards of the Turkish front line trench at the Krithia nullah.

On November 27th a severe storm started. The difficulties

of remaining in this precarious position, where troops were dependent on sea-borne supplies, were now being realized.

The storm of November 27th was followed by twelve hours' rain without intermission; then there was a north wind and snow blizzard for three days. In the following week 10,000 sick were evacuated.

By the second week in December over 96,000 cases had been admitted to hospital since the beginning of the campaign.

In the past seven months 25,000 had died, 12,000 were missing, and 75,000 had been wounded.

General Monro's duty now was, as he pointed out in his despatches, dated March 6th, 1916:—

1. To report on the military situation in the Gallipoli Peninsula.

2. To give an opinion: as to how many troops would be required (i) to capture and hold the Peninsula; (ii) to keep the Straits open; (iii) to capture Constantinople.

3. To state whether the Peninsula should be evacuated or not.

General Monro gave a clearly expressed opinion as to the advisability of evacuating the Peninsula before the winter set in.

CHAPTER XII.

THE EVACUATION.

THE difficulties of an evacuation from the Peninsula would be as follows:—

Three Army Corps had to be embarked. This was not possible at one time with our existing shipping. The weather might at any moment interfere with the embarkation after it had started.

The Turks, who had all the advantages of observation, would be able to see the preparations being made for embarkation, and would be able to add to its difficulties by interfering with its progress.

In his despatches, General Monro expressed his opinion on this subject as follows:—

"The position occupied by our troops presented a military situation unique in history. The mere fringe of the coast line had been secured. The beaches and piers, upon which they were dependent for all requirements in personnel and material, were exposed to registered and observed artillery fire. Our entrenchments were dominated almost throughout by the Turks.

"The possible artillery positions were insufficient and defective. The force, in short, held a line possessing every military defect. The position was without depth, the communications were insecure and dependent on the weather. No means existed for the concealment and deployment of fresh troops destined for the offensive; whilst the Turks enjoyed full powers of observation, abundant artillery positions, and they had been given the time to supplement the natural advantages which the position presented by all the devices at the disposal of the Field Engineer."

The difficulty for the War Council that still remained to be solved was that the naval authorities were unwilling to agree to the evacuation of Helles; as General Monro had advocated definitely that the whole Peninsula should be evacuated. His conclusion was as follows:—" Since we could not hope to achieve any purpose by remaining on the Peninsula, the appalling cost to the nation involved in consequence of embarking on an overseas expedition with no base available for the rapid transit of stores, supplies and personnel, made it urgent that we should divert the troops locked up on the Peninsula to a more useful theatre."

Lord Kitchener accordingly was despatched to the Ægean to review the situation and inspect positions held by the troops. He endorsed General Monro's opinion.

On December 8th orders were sent to the Commander-in-Chief to withdraw his forces from Anzac and Suvla. The troops at Helles were to be left there.

The Navy wanted Helles to be retained by the Army, as that would prevent the Turks from placing guns to fire seawards from Cape Tekke, Cape Helles, Sedd-el-Bahr, or Eski Hissarlik Point.

It was decided that this operation for the evacuation of Anzac and Suvla should be finally concluded on the night of December 19th/20th.

General Monro considered that it should be carried out in three stages. During the first stage all troops, animals and supplies not required for the actual conduct of operations were to be withdrawn gradually by night from December 10th to the 17th.

During the second stages, on the night of December 18th/19th, all troops, approximately 11,000, guns and stores not then required would be embarked.

In the final stage, between darkness and dawn, on the night of December 19th/20th, the remaining troops, approximately 11,000 men, and material were to be embarked as rapidly as possible.

The normal routine was to be maintained during daylight, including the usual shelling and bursts of machine-gun fire.

New lines of trenches and wire entanglements were to be constructed to cover the lines of withdrawal and the embarkation points in case a rearguard action became necessary.

At Suvla the beaches were five miles from the enemy's position, and open throughout to the Turks' fire and observation.

At Anzac the beaches were more concealed, but they were less than two miles from the Turkish positions. Therefore only a keep was prepared for use if required at Anzac Cove. During the period of preparation for evacuation the Turks, fortunately, were unusually quiet.

Heavy guns from Germany were being placed in position, and this occupation appeared to keep employed the 20,000 Turks holding the forward positions at Anzac and Suvla.

The Turks were apparently completely misled by the fact that the shelling by day was the same, although the number of guns was reduced.

THE DARDANELLES CAMPAIGN 75

The weather throughout was favourable, so that extra piers could be constructed.

At Suvla the area was divided into two sectors: one north of the Salt Lake for embarkation between new Pier and Suvla Cove, and one south of the Salt Lake for embarkation northeast and south-east of Nibrunesi Point at South Pier and "C" Beach.

The second line of defence ran practically north and south through Hill 10. Lala Baba was specially fortified as a keep.

It was expected, however, that troops should proceed direct to the beach from their trenches, and that these positions should not be occupied except in cases of emergency.

At Anzac the removals were carried out by night from Ocean Beach. The forward positions were held by the 2nd Australian Division, Yeomanry and 29th Indian Infantry Brigade up to and including Hill 60.

Embarkation started with a gradual withdrawal from the flanks at both areas at 2000 hours on the night of December 19th/20th.

At both areas the front line trenches were held by detachments until 0130 hours. At 0230 hours Chatham Post was evacuated. At 0300 hours troops left Lone Pine and Pope's, Quinn's and Courtney's Posts half an hour later. Fifteen minutes after these posts had been evacuated a series of mines were exploded at the head of Monash Gully, and that was the first intimation the Turks had that anything unusual was happening. So great apparently was the Turks' surprise that when this mine was exploded by the Anzacs by electric contact from a distance they evidently expected an attack, and for forty minutes continued rapid fire at empty trenches.

By 0415 hours the embarkation had been successfully completed, and there had only been three casualties.

Four eighteen-pounder guns, two five-inch howitzers, one 4.7-inch gun, an anti-aircraft gun, and two three-pounder Hotchkiss guns were left behind after they had been rendered unserviceable. Also some damaged vehicles and stores could not be taken away.

At Suvla the embarkations were completed by 0530 hours. The Turks, as at Anzac, were inactive. The last detachments were able to march straight to the beaches through the support lines. All animals, guns, and stores were embarked.

The whole operation had been carried so well and easily exactly as it had been planned that it was doubtful if another evacuation could be equally successful.

However, orders were received on December 28th to

evacuate the Helles area, with 40,000 men, 4,500 animals and 150 guns.

Marshal Liman von Sanders now had twenty-one divisions to deal with four British divisions at Helles. The Turks also had a great superiority in artillery and ammunition.

The French infantry were the first to be relieved by troops who had been at Suvla, and who were resting at Imbros and Lemnos.

As at Suvla, defensive positions were prepared to cover the embarkation points. These positions were from de Tott's Battery to Gully Beach and from Sedd-el-Bahr to "X" Beach. A keep was constructed to cover Cape Tekke.

The evacuation was methodically carried out on the same lines as those, which had been successful at Anzac and Suvla.

The fighting force was gradually reduced until, on the final night of January 8th/9th, detachments only would be left holding the front line trenches. These last detachments were to leave their trenches at 2345 hours, and to reach "V," "W" and Gully Beaches an hour later.

In order to deceive the enemy, bombing and machine gun and rifle fire was carried out nightly until 2330 hours, when all was quiet again.

The Turks became accustomed to this routine, and consequently suspected nothing unusual on the night of our actual departure, although the Turks were more alert than they had been during the withdrawals from Anzac and Suvla.

Many casualties were incurred at the beaches owing to the heavy shelling, as the Turkish Staff were aware of the possibility of evacuation, although they did not foresee the actual date of departure.

The instructions for the evacuation, as given in the naval despatches, dated January 26th, 1916, were as follows:—

"(a) The withdrawal should be conducted with the utmost rapidity, the final stage being limited to one night.

"(b) Every effort should be made to improve embarkation facilities at as many points on the coast as could be used, other than 'W' and 'V' Beaches.

"(c) Forty-eight hours before the evacuation was completed the number of men remaining on the Peninsula was to be cut down to 22,000. Of these, 7,000 were to embark on the last night but one, leaving 15,000 for the final night. At the request of the military the latter number was increased to 17,000. As few guns as possible were to be left to the final night, and arrangements were made to destroy any of these which it might be found impossible to remove, or which, by

THE DARDANELLES CAMPAIGN

reason of their condition, were considered not worth removing."

By the night of January 1st/2nd, 1916, all the French Infantry had been relieved.

The further progress of events was handicapped by bad weather. High winds interrupted embarkation for long periods. Then on "V" Beach a French battleship collided with and sank a British transport which was about to embark a thousand mules, with the result that finally 568 had to be left in the Peninsula.

Intermediate posts on the lines of withdrawal to "V" Beach, "W" Beach, and Gully Beach were arranged and connected by telephone.

By January 8th, 16,918 and 54 guns were left to be embarked.

It was decided that, with the exception of 400 men of the 13th Division and some beach personnel at Gully Beach, the whole force should be embarked at "W" and "V" Beaches after dark on January 8th.

The only means by which the Turks could hope to find out if the troops from Helles were to be withdrawn or not from the Peninsula was to attack in force, as the usual appearance of the beaches and back areas was maintained throughout the day, and the artillery, as at Anzac and Suvla, continued to use the normal expenditure of ammunition with reduced numbers of guns.

All traffic was continued on the roads as usual. Tents remained pitched. Stores were withdrawn from the centre of their blocks, and the holes left were covered with tarpaulins. Animals, stores and war material were removed on successive nights.

The arduous work of the Royal Engineers and the labour parties under their direction was one of the chief factors of success in this embarkation in keeping the pier facilities sufficiently intact to enable the Navy to carry out their rôle in the general plan.

The difficulty was to carry out an adequate defence if storms suddenly started after the first batches of troops had left the Peninsula.

The Navy estimated that they could not embark more than 15,000 in one night. The G.O.C. estimated that he could not resist attack in his present positions with less than 22,000 and 60 guns.

This would necessitate embarkation on two nights. Actually 2,300 men and nine guns were embarked on the night January 7th/8th. It was therefore decided to embark 17,000 men and 40 guns on zero, minus one day, and the remainder on the zero day. The force was then to be gradually reduced until the forward lines were held by two-thirds of their strength in rifles and machine guns, and until batteries became finally one gun.

A support line running across the Peninsula parallel to the front line and a mile behind it was dug and strengthened.

This was held by small groups at points where communication trenches leading to " V," " W " and Gully Beaches were.

The right-half of the British line was to withdraw by " V " Beach and the left-half by " W " Beach, except for a final detachment, which was to leave by Gully Beach.

Another line of posts a mile further back was established between de Tott's Battery and Gully Beach. Behind this line the R.N., 52nd, 29th and 13th Divisions arranged a rendezvous, where they formed up and marched to the embarkation zone behind the beach defences, stretching from Sedd-el-Bahr to the coast north-west of Hill 114.

The Turks remained unusually quiet in their trenches until January 7th, as the VIII Corps continued to maintain an offensive attitude by bombing, sniping and raids.

At midday on the front of the 12th Turkish Division, opposed to our 13th Division on the left of our line, a violent bombardment was directed mainly against Gully Spur. It was continued for five hours. Considerable damage was done to the forward and communication trenches, but the attack by the Turkish infantry did not materialize in strength.

An attack on the coast at Fusilier Bluff was driven back with heavy loss.

Our losses were 6 officers and 158 other ranks.

The Turks did not appear to realize or to gain any information as to how weakly our lines were held.

Embarkation during the night of January 7th/8th was successfully carried out, leaving the troops only to be embarked in accordance with the plan. By this time rather more than half the troops had left the Peninsula.

January 8th was calm until 1600 hours, when the wind changed to the south-west.

For the final phase on the night of January 8th/9th, it was decided that the timings for departure should be from " W " and " V " beaches at 2000 hours for the first troops.

The second batch of troops should be on board by 2130 hours, and all the remainder by 0300 hours.

The Turks remained quiet throughout the day, but the wind gradually grew stronger during the evening. By 2100 hours half a gale was blowing from the west and south-west. In spite of this, the embarkation continued. The last detachment

THE DARDANELLES CAMPAIGN

left the trenches at 2345 hours without the Turks noticing their departure. This was possible owing to the Turks sending out no patrols to find out if the trenches opposite to them had been vacated or not.

It was not until 0220 hours that any serious accident occurred. At this time a lighter ran aground at Gully Beach, and could not be refloated. The troops at this beach then marched to " W " Beach, arriving there by 0345 hours, just in time to embark before the heavy seas and surf made it impossible from the weakening piers.

Just before the last boats left the shore the large quantities of stores left behind were set on fire.

The Turks then became aware that once more the British troops on their front had eluded them.

Up to this date, in the eight months' operations on the Peninsula the total casualties had been 117,549, of which 28,200 had been killed. In addition, 96,683 sick were admitted to hospital by the middle of December.

The Prime Minister in the House of Commons, on January 10th, 1916, reported to the members that the retirement would take an imperishable place in our national history.

Certainly the success of the evacuation was due to excellent staff work and to co-operation between the Navy and the Army.

General Monro's special order after the evacuation stated that: " The arrangements made for withdrawal and for keeping the enemy in ignorance of the operation that was taking place could not have been improved. It is no exaggeration to call this achievement one without parallel. To disengage and to withdraw from a bold and active enemy is the most difficult of all military operations, and in this case the withdrawal was effected by surprise, with the opposing forces at close grips—in many cases within a few yards of each other. Such an operation, when succeeded by a re-embarkation from an open beach, is one for which military history contains no precedent. No soldier relishes undertaking a withdrawal from before the enemy.

" It is hard to leave behind the graves of good comrades and to relinquish positions so hardly won and so gallantly maintained as those we left. But all ranks in the Dardanelles army will realize that in this matter they were but carrying out the orders of His Majesty's Government, so that they might in due course be more usefully employed in fighting elsewhere for their King, their country, and the Empire."

CHAPTER XIII.

Troops engaged in the Gallipoli Campaign:—
FRENCH CORPS.
1st Division.

1st Metropolitan Brigade—
  175th Regiment.
  Composite Regiment of 1st Bn. Foreign Legion.
  2nd Bn. Zouaves.

2nd Colonial Brigade—
  4th Colonial Regiment.
  6th Colonial Regiment.

2nd Division.

3rd Metropolitan Brigade—
  176th Regiment.
  2nd African Regiment (three Battalions Zouaves).

4th Colonial Brigade—
  7th Colonial Regiment.
  8th Colonial Regiment.

Two Regiments—
  Chasseurs d'Afrique.

ANZAC CORPS.
1st Australian Division.

1st Australian Brigade—
  1st New South Wales Battalion.
  2nd New South Wales Battalion.
  3rd New South Wales Battalion.
  4th New South Wales Battalion.

2nd Australian Brigade—
  5th Victoria Battalion.
  6th Victoria Battalion.
  7th Victoria Battalion.
  8th Victoria Battalion.

3rd *Australian Brigade*—
    9th Queensland Battalion.
    10th South Australian Battalion.
    11th West Australian Battalion.
    12th South and West Australian and Tasmania Battalion.

NEW ZEALAND AND AUSTRALIAN DIVISION.

New Zealand Brigade—
    Auckland Battalion.
    Canterbury Battalion.
    Otago Battalion.
    Wellington Battalion.

4th *Australian Brigade*—
    13th New South Wales Battalion.
    14th Victoria Battalion.
    15th Queensland and Tasmania Battalion.
    16th South and West Australian Battalion.

New Zealand Mounted Rifle Brigade—
    Auckland Mounted Rifles.
    Canterbury Mounted Rifles.
    Wellington Mounted Rifles.

1st *Australian Light Horse Brigade*—
    1st New South Wales Regiment.
    2nd Queensland Regiment.
    3rd South Australian and Tasmania Regiment.

2ND AUSTRALIAN DIVISION.

5th *Australian Brigade*—
    17th New South Wales Battalion.
    18th New South Wales Battalion.
    19th New South Wales Battalion.
    20th New South Wales Battalion.

6th *Australian Brigade*—
    21st Victoria Battalion.
    22nd Victoria Battalion.
    23rd Victoria Battalion.
    24th Victoria Battalion.

7th Australian Brigade—
    25th Queensland Battalion.
    26th Queensland and Tasmania Battalion.
    27th South Australia Battalion.
    28th West Australia Battalion.

Divisional Troops—
    13th (Victoria) Light Horse Regiment.

Corps Troops.

2nd Australian Light Horse Brigade—
    5th Queensland Regiment.
    6th New South Wales Regiment.
    7th New South Wales Regiment.

3rd Australian Light Horse Brigade—
    8th Victoria Regiment.
    9th Victoria and South Australia Regiment.
    10th West Australia Regiment.

Attached New Zealand and Australian Division.

29th Indian Infantry Brigade—
    14th Sikhs.
    1st/5th Gurkha Rifles.
    1st/6th Gurkha Rifles.
    2nd/10th Gurkha Rifles.

VIII CORPS.
29th Division.

86th Brigade—
    2nd Royal Fusiliers.
    1st Lancashire Fusiliers.
    1st Royal Munster Fusiliers.
    1st Royal Dublin Fusiliers.

87th Brigade—
    2nd South Wales Borderers.
    1st King's Own Scottish Borderers.
    1st Royal Inniskilling Fusiliers.
    1st Border Regiment.

THE DARDANELLES CAMPAIGN

88th Brigade—
    2nd Hampshire Regiment.
    4th Worcestershire Regiment.
    1st Essex Regiment.
    5th Royal Scots.

The Newfoundland Battalion joined the 88th Brigade in September; 2nd/3rd and 2nd/1st London Regiments joined the 29th Division on September 24th.

42ND EAST LANCASHIRE DIVISION.

125th Brigade—
    5th Lancashire Fusiliers.
    6th Lancashire Fusiliers.
    7th Lancashire Fusiliers.
    8th Lancashire Fusiliers.

126th Brigade—
    4th East Lancashire Regiment.
    5th East Lancashire Regiment.
    9th Manchester Regiment.
    10th Manchester Regiment.

127th Brigade—
    5th Manchester Regiment.
    6th Manchester Regiment.
    7th Manchester Regiment.
    8th Manchester Regiment.

52ND LOWLAND DIVISION.

155th Brigade—
    4th Royal Scots Fusiliers.
    5th Royal Scots Fusiliers.
    4th King's Own Scottish Borderers.
    5th King's Own Scottish Borderers.

156th Brigade—
    4th Royal Scots.
    7th Royal Scots.
    7th Scottish Rifles.
    8th Scottish Rifles.

157th Brigade—
    5th Highland Light Infantry.
    6th Highland Light Infantry.
    7th Highland Light Infantry.
    5th Argyll and Sutherland Highlanders.

ROYAL NAVAL DIVISION.

1st Naval Brigade—
    Drake Battalion.
    Nelson Battalion.
    Hawke Battalion.
    Hood Battalion.

2nd Naval Brigade—
    1st Bn. Royal Marine Light Infantry.
    2nd Bn. Royal Marine Light Infantry.
    Howe Battalion.
    Anson Battalion.

IX CORPS.

10TH (IRISH) DIVISION.

29th Brigade—
    10th Hampshire Regiment.
    6th Royal Irish Rifles.
    5th Connaught Rangers.
    6th Leinster Regiment.

30th Brigade—
    6th Royal Dublin Fusiliers.
    7th Royal Dublin Fusiliers.
    6th Royal Munster Fusiliers.
    7th Royal Munster Fusiliers.

31st Brigade—
    5th Royal Inniskilling Fusiliers.
    6th Royal Inniskilling Fusiliers.
    5th Royal Irish Fusiliers.
    6th Royal Irish Fusiliers.

Divisional Battalion—
    5th Royal Irish Regiment.

11TH DIVISION.

32nd Brigade—
   9th West Yorkshire Regiment.
   6th West Yorkshire Regiment.
   8th West Riding Regiment.
   6th York and Lancaster Regiment.

33rd Brigade—
   6th Lincolnshire Regiment.
   6th Border Regiment.
   7th South Staffordshire Regiment.
   9th Sherwood Foresters.

34th Brigade—
   8th Northumberland Fusiliers.
   9th Lancashire Fusiliers.
   5th Dorsetshire Regiment.
   11th Manchester Regiment.

Divisional Battalion—
   6th East Yorkshire Regiment.

13TH DIVISION.

38th Brigade—
   6th King's Own Regiment.
   6th East Lancashire Regiment.
   6th South Lancashire Regiment.
   6th Loyal North Lancashire Regiment.

39th Brigade—
   9th Warwickshire Regiment.
   9th Gloucestershire Regiment.
   9th Worcestershire Regiment.
   7th North Staffordshire Regiment.

40th Brigade—
   4th South Wales Borderers.
   8th Royal Welch Fusiliers.
   8th Cheshire Regiment.
   5th Wiltshire Regiment.

Divisional Battalion—
   8th Welch Regiment.

53RD DIVISION.

158th Brigade—
    5th Royal Welch Fusiliers.
    6th Royal Welch Fusiliers.
    7th Royal Welch Fusiliers.
    1st Herefordshire Regiment.

159th Brigade—
    4th Cheshire Regiment.
    7th Cheshire Regiment.
    4th Welch Regiment.
    5th Welch Regiment.

160th Brigade—
    4th Queen's Regiment.
    4th Royal Sussex Regiment.
    4th Royal West Kent Regiment.
    10th Middlesex Regiment.

Divisional Battalion—
    1st Welch Regiment.

54TH DIVISION.

161st Brigade.
    4th Essex Regiment.
    5th Essex Regiment.
    6th Essex Regiment.
    7th Essex Regiment.

162nd Brigade—
    5th Bedfordshire Regiment.
    4th Northamptonshire Regiment.
    10th London Regiment.
    11th London Regiment.

163rd Brigade—
    4th Norfolk Regiment.
    5th Norfolk Regiment.
    5th Suffolk Regiment.
    8th Hampshire Regiment.

2ND MOUNTED DIVISION.

1st South Midland Brigade—
>Warwickshire Yeomanry.
>Worcestershire Yeomanry.
>Gloucestershire Hussars.

2nd South Midland Brigade—
>Buckinghamshire Hussars.
>Berkshire Yeomanry.
>Dorset Yeomanry.

3rd Notts and Derby Brigade—
>Sherwood Rangers.
>South Notts Hussars.
>Derbyshire Yeomanry.

4th London Brigade—
>1st County of London Yeomanry.
>1st City of London Yeomanry.
>3rd County of London Yeomanry.

Divisional Regiments—
>Hertfordshire Yeomanry.
>Westminster Dragoons.

New Zealand Mounted Brigade (arrived May 12th)—
>Auckland Mounted Rifles.
>Canterbury Mounted Rifles.
>Wellington Mounted Rifles.
>Otago Mounted Rifles.

Scottish Horse Brigade (arrived early in September)—
>1/1st Scottish Horse.
>2/1st Scottish Horse.
>3/1st Scottish Horse.

Highland Mounted Brigade (arrived last week in September), attached to 2nd Mounted Division—
>1st Lovat's Scouts.
>2nd Lovat's Scouts.
>Fife and Forfar Yeomanry.

South Western Mounted Brigade (arrived October 9th), attached 11th Division—
  Devon Yeomanry.
  Devon Hussars.
  West Somerset Yeomanry.

South Eastern Mounted Brigade (arrived during October), attached 42nd Division—
  East Kent Mounted Rifles.
  West Kent Yeomanry.
  Sussex Yeomanry.

Lowland Mounted Brigade (arrived during October), attached 52nd Division—
  Ayrshire Yeomanry.
  Lanark Yeomanry.

CHAPTER XIV.

List of Dates.

September 4th to June 6th.

1914.

September 4th.—The Secretary of State for Foreign Affairs instructed the British minister at Athens that if Turkey joined the Central Powers, Greece should be encouraged to become our ally.

November 2nd.—Russia declared war on Turkey.

November 3rd.—French and British ships carried out long range bombardment against the forts at the entrance to the Dardanelles.

November 5th.—France and Britain formally declared war on Turkey.

November 18th.—The *Goeben* was damaged in a naval battle.

December 13th.—Our submarine B11 entered the Straits of Gallipoli and torpedoed a Turkish warship.

December 14th.—The Serbians recaptured Belgrade. Greece and Roumania decided to remain neutral unless Bulgaria attacked Turkey.

December 28th.—The Commander-in-Chief in France reported that the Allies' line on the Western Front was now secure. Another area for Britain's efforts was, therefore, considered.

The French Government considered that the correct strategy for the Allies was to concentrate all available strength on the Western Front.

1915—

January 2nd.—The Commander-in-Chief of the Russian Army asked that either a naval or a military demonstration might be made in order to ease the situation in the Caucasus.

January 3rd.—Lord Fisher urged that an attack should be made on Turkey immediately from Besika Bay by British and Indian troops, by the Greeks from the Gallipoli Peninsula and by the Bulgarians from Adrianople, while our ships forced the Dardanelles. Demonstrations were also to be made at Haifa and Alexandretta, where it was suggested a landing should be made.

January 7th.—The War Council vetoed Sir John French's plan for an advance on Zeebrugge in conjunction with the fleet.

THE DARDANELLES CAMPAIGN

January 8th.—Lord Kitchener suggested that an attack should be made with 150,000 troops in co-operation with the fleet against the Dardanelles.

January 11th.—Admiral Carden's detailed plan for forcing the Dardanelles by ships was received by the War Council. This plan was a gradual reduction of the forts at the entrance to the Dardanelles, then of the inside defences, then of those at the Narrows; and finally clearing the minefields guarding the entrance to the sea of Marmora.

January 13th.—Our successful naval action off the Dogger Bank removed many of the apprehensions of a successful landing by the Germans on the east coast. The War Council were able to consider the use of available troops in England for operations in the Dardanelles.

January 15th.—The Government approved of the general principle of Admiral Carden's scheme.

January 19th.—Russia was informed that an attempt would be made to force the Dardanelles.

January 23rd.—The British Minister in Athens offered concessions to the Greek Government in Asia Minor if Greece became an ally of the Serbians.

January 28th.—The War Council instructed the Admiralty to undertake a naval attack on the Dardanelles.

February 6th.—Two marine battalions were sent to Mudros Harbour in the island of Lemnos to act as landing parties during the naval operations.

February 9th.—Bulgaria obtained a loan from Germany. This was an indication that Bulgaria would join the Central Powers.

February 15th.—The Greek Government rejected the offer of a reinforcement to their army of a British and a French division. The idea of the Salonika expedition was, therefore, temporarily given up.

February 16th.—The War Council decided to send the 29th Division as early as possible to Mudros. Orders were also given for the military forces in Egypt to be available to support the Navy in their attack on the Dardanelles.

February 18th.—The French Government decided to send a division for operations to the Eastern Mediterranean. Marshal Joffre would not consent to spare a division from his command.

February 19th.—Lord Kitchener cancelled the decision to send the 29th Division to the Dardanelles. The Australian and New Zealand divisions were to be sent from Egypt instead.

Five British and three French ships bombarded the forts at the entrance to the Dardanelles.

THE DARDANELLES CAMPAIGN

No serious damage was done to the Turks' fortifications.

February 23rd.—Transports had been collected in Egypt for carrying one brigade to Mudros.

February 24th.—The War Council decided that the army should, if required, help to carry out the Dardanelles operations.

February 25th.—Ten battleships renewed the bombardment on the Turks' outer forts, whose guns were temporarily silenced.

February 26th.—Three battleships entered the Dardanelles and shelled the intermediate defences of the Narrows. Land guns and howitzers, which were unlocated, replied effectively. Marines landed at Kum Kale and Sedd-el-Bahr.

March 1st.—Four battleships again bombarded the intermediate defences of the Narrows. The result was inconclusive.

A landing party at Kum Kale, from H.M.S. *Irresistible* destroyed guns and a searchlight there.

March 4th.—Two companies of the Plymouth Battalion were brought over respectively to Kum Kale and Sedd-el-Bahr from Imbros.

At both places the Turks were alert and strongly opposed our advance. At neither of these places could the objective be gained.

It was now estimated that there were 40,000 Turks in the vicinity of the Straits.

Admiral Carden reported to the Admiralty that the fleet would probably be through the Narrows soon after March 16th, and suggested that the available troops should be ready for operations at Mudros by that date.

March 5th.—The outer forts of Smyrna were bombarded.

March 6th.—Dardanus and Soghandere forts were bombarded. Also the Chanak and Kilid Bahr forts were bombarded from the Gulf of Saros. The results were not substantial.

March 10th.—Turkish defences at Bulair and at Morto Bay were bombarded.

Lord Kitchener promised to send the 29th Division to the Ægean for operations in the Dardanelles campaign.

March 11th.—French warships shelled the Bulair lines. British warships bombarded the Turkish defences at Morto Bay.

The Russian Black Sea fleet approached the Bosphorus and sank many Turkish steamers.

General Sir Ian Hamilton was appointed to command the Allied troops in the Mediterranean. Lord Kitchener considered that 75,000 men would be sufficient to carry out the operation which he was to undertake, as the Turks were busily engaged elsewhere.

March 13th.—Sir Ian Hamilton, with his Staff, left London to command the Mediterranean Expeditionary Force.

March 15th.—The Admiralty agreed to a general fleet attack being undertaken against the defences of the Narrows.

March 17th.—Sir Ian Hamilton and Staff arrived at Tenedos. At a conference at which the Commander of the French troops and Admiral de Robeck were present it was decided that the Navy should attempt to get through the Dardanelles without the help of the Army.

March 18th.—The naval attack on the Narrows took place. Three battleships were lost and three others were very badly damaged in this operation.

At dusk our ships left the Straits and had not silenced the forts at the Narrows.

This was the last attempt made by the Navy to try to force the Dardanelles.

The Commander-in-Chief suggested that Alexandria should become the base for the Mediterranean Expeditionary Force.

March 22nd.—The transports were sent to Alexandria to be repacked so that what was first required by troops on disembarking would be most easily and quickly accessible.

The Commander-in-Chief and Admiral de Robeck both concurred in the opinion that the fleet would require the assistance of the Army to force the Dardanelles; and that the whole force assembled in the Ægean would be required for the operation.

March 24th.—Sir Ian Hamilton and his Staff left Mudros for Alexandria.

The first plan for a landing was considered.

General d'Amade suggested that a landing should be made on the Asiatic coast near Besika.

Our plan included a landing at the southern end of the Peninsula by the 29th Division and the French Division, and in addition a landing by the Anzac Corps north of Jaba Tepe. Feints were to be made at Bulair.

March 27th.—Royal Naval Division arrived at Port Said.

March 28th.—29th Division and French troops arrived at Alexandria.

Our troops were armed and equipped for mobile warfare. Ammunition reserves were not ample, and in addition the S.A.A. used for the rifles of the 29th Division could not be used by the Royal Naval Division.

April 6th.—Lord Kitchener directed the Commander of the troops in Egypt to supply any troops that could be spared for the Gallipoli campaign.

THE DARDANELLES CAMPAIGN 93

April 8th.—The Commander-in-Chief and the General Staff left for Mudros.

April 16th.—Since April 4th forty-five transports had been sent to Mudros from Alexandria.

April 19th.—Instructions for landing at Helles were issued to the 29th Division.

The main attack was to be made by this Division from three beaches to capture Achi Baba and then the Kilid Bahr plateau.

The flanks of the troops landing at these three beaches were to be protected by two additional landings on either flank in order to threaten the Turks opposing our main landings with envelopment.

The 29th Division was also informed that there would be demonstrations at Bulair and Besika Bay, and that French troops would land at Kum Kale and that the Anzac troops would advance towards the Narrows from the vicinity of a landing-place north of Gaba Tepe.

The first contingent to land at the southern beaches " S," " V," " W," " X " and " Y," were 4,900 men. Shortly afterwards 3,300 men were to arrive. At the vicinity of Gaba Tepe a covering force of 4,000 men was to be landed for the capture of the Sari Bair spurs near their landing-place. Then the remainder of the Anzac Corps was to land and capture the high ground—Mal Tepe—overlooking the Narrows.

Another attack by the fleet was to be undertaken against the defences of the Narrows.

April 17th.—Submarine E15, in attempting to get through to the Sea of Marmora, ran aground near Kephez Point. In order to render this submarine useless to the enemy it was torpedoed during the night.

April 23rd.—It was estimated that the Turks in the Gallipoli area were 45,000 rifles. Their Commander, General Liman von Sanders, disposed them as follows: The 5th and 7th Turkish Divisions were in the vicinity of the isthmus of Bulair. The 9th Division was distributed between Suvla Bay and Sedd-el-Bahr. The 3rd and 11th Divisions were in the Asiatic shore from Kum Kale to Besika Bay. The 19th Division was in reserve at Boghali.

The Turks actually defending the Anzac landing place were one company, with another in support. At " V," " W " and " X " beaches they had two forward companies, with two companies and a company of engineers in reserve. They had no troops at " Y " beach. The nearest troops to this beach were two platoons at the mouth of Gully Ravine. One company was holding positions round Morto Bay, with one platoon at " S " beach.

At Kum Kale and Yeni Shehr the Turks had one regiment near the coast.

April 25th.—Two brigades of the Royal Naval Division escorted by three warships took up a position in the Gulf of Saros. The Bulair lines were bombarded soon after daybreak. Later in the day troops were sent in boats towards the shore and later returned to their transports.

The Anzac Corps was to land a mile north of Gaba Tepe and then, after securing the ground gained, to advance on Maidos, and thus to cut the Turks' communications from north to south.

The covering force was to occupy a position on Chunuk Bair, 3,000 yards from the coast at Fisherman's Hut, and also to capture 400-foot Plateau.

At 0425 hours, fifty yards from the beach the twelve tows carrying the covering force were cast off towards the shore, a mile north of the intended landing-place.

This was lucky from the point of view of the opposition encountered, as there were only a sentry group on Ari Burnu and a few small posts on the ridge overlooking the beach.

On the other hand the difficulty of the country in their front was considerable, and it was not easy to know how to carry out their original orders in unknown, unreconnoitred country.

The second trip brought the remainder of the covering force ashore by 0440 hours. This force occupied positions on 400 Plateau and Pine Ridge.

At 0600 the 2nd Australian Brigade landed and occupied positions on the right of the covering force on Bolton's Ridge.

Actually some troops advanced to Scrubby Knoll from where they could see the Narrows.

By 1300 hours the Turks were 20,000 strong.

By 1630 hours 13,000 men were ashore, and one mountain battery. By 1800 hours three Australian Brigades and half a New Zealand Brigade were ashore.

The Turks made three counter-attacks during the day, which were successfully checked with the co-operation of our warships. It was necessary to re-organize the forces and to consolidate on a line running in a semi-circle with the left flank on the high ground east of Fisherman's Hut and the right flank a mile north of Gaba Tepe.

During the night the Turks' counter-attacks were continued without material success.

Ammunition and water supply were a source of anxiety and the actual position that was being held by the troops

THE DARDANELLES CAMPAIGN

had little depth, so that the Commander at Anzac suggested evacuation of the area to the Commander-in-Chief.

Instructions were sent to General Birdwood to hold on to his position at Anzac.

Helles: At "S" Beach three companies of the 2nd South Wales Borderers, supported by the fire of H.M.S. *Cornwallis* and H.M.S. *Lord Nelson*, were able to gain a position on the high ground near de Totts' battery. This ground was held by this detachment until April 27th, when touch was obtained with the troops who landed at "V" beach.

At "V" beach H.M.S. *Albion* bombarded the beach and Turkish positions, and H.M.S. *Queen Elizabeth* bombarded Sedd-el-Bahr. Then three companies of Dublin Fusiliers were towed ashore, half a company of which landed at Camber Beach, east of Sedd-el-Bahr. These troops were followed by the *River Clyde*, containing the remainder of the Dublin Fusiliers, the Munster Fusiliers, two companies of the Hampshire Regiment and a field company R.E.

When the boats transporting the Dublin Fusiliers reached the shore the *River Clyde* unfortunately ran aground further out to sea than had been anticipated.

There was difficulty, owing to the strong tide, in arranging the lighters, which were to form a pier between the ship and the shore.

The Turks opened a very heavy fire on the boats at the time when the *River Clyde* grounded.

When two companies had reached the beach the lighters broke adrift and there was much delay in rectifying the situation and in reinforcing those who had landed. The machine guns placed in the ship's bows prevented the Turks from concentrating their fire on, or from counter-attacking, the troops, who had found some cover behind a sand bank on the beach.

By 1100 hours nearly a thousand men of the Hampshire Regiment and of the Munster Fusiliers had been able to reach the beach from the *River Clyde*, although they had fifty per cent casualties.

During the night the Turks holding the ruined fort and village of Sedd-el-Bahr were attacked. Owing to the exhaustion of our troops and the bright moonlight, which enabled the Turks to gain full advantage from their concealed posts, these positions were not captured until 1000 hours on April 26th.

Hill 141, north-west of Sedd-el-Bahr, was captured by 1400 hours on this day.

The troops that had landed at Camber Beach were

re-embarked, as they had suffered heavily and were unable to advance to their first objective:—the village of Sedd-el-Bahr.

At "W" Beach the 1st Battalion Lancashire Fusiliers were brought on board the *Euryalus* and then transferred to cutters, which were towed towards the shore by picket-boats. They reached the beach at 0600 hours. The beach and cliffs had been bombarded by our warships since 0500 hours.

The landing was made in three parties. One party landed under Cape Tekke, another party landed on the beach near Cape Helles, and the central party gained a position at the southern side of Hill 114.

When this latter party was reinforced by the Worcestershire Regiment they were able to effect a junction on Hill 114 with the Royal Fusiliers, who had landed at "X" Beach.

Those who had landed on the beach near Cape Helles were strongly opposed by the Turks covering their wire obstacles with machine-gun and rifle fire.

After these obstacles had been heavily bombarded by our ships, an attack was made in co-operation with the Worcesters against Hill 138. By 1600 hours a position on this hill was gained, but touch was not obtained on the right with the troops who had landed at "V" beach.

A line, however, was gained by the evening from the east of Cape Helles' lighthouse, through Hill 138 to Hill 114. Twelve and a half battalions were ashore in the Helles area by this time.

At "X" Beach the 1st Battalion Royal Fusiliers landed from H.M.S. *Implacable*, covered by the fire from the *Swiftsure* and *Implacable*.

An attempt was made as soon as the top of the cliffs had been reached to gain contact with the Lancashire Fusiliers at "W" Beach, at Hill 114. This was accomplished before nightfall with the support of the Border Regiment and Inniskilling Fusiliers.

At "Y" Beach the K.O.S.B. landed without difficulty and reached the top of the cliffs on their front without opposition, followed by the Plymouth Battalion of the Royal Naval Division. These troops were unable to join up with the Royal Fusiliers at "X" Beach. Their isolated position might have become untenable, and consequently on April 26th they were re-embarked.

At Kum Kale the French troops considerably assisted the main operations by capturing the village and by preventing the Turks from enfilading the landing parties by their fire from the fort at Kum Kale.

April 26th.—The Commander-in-Chief ordered a French

THE DARDANELLES CAMPAIGN 97

Brigade to be sent to "X" Beach. By the evening a continuous line from Sedd-el-Bahr to Beach "X" was in our hands through Hills 114 and 138.

Turkish reinforcements were slow in arriving in the Helles area during this day.

There were only five Turkish battalions in the area south of Achi Baba.

At Anzac the ground captured was organized into brigade areas. The 2nd Australian Brigade occupied a position from Bolton's Ridge to the centre of the 400 Plateau. The 1st and 3rd Australian Brigades continued the positions to Quinn's Post and then back to the sea through the middle of Russell's Top and the Walker's Ridge spur; with a detachment from the 4th Australian Brigade on Pope's Hill, between Quinn's Post and Russell's Top.

Except for an attempt by the 4th Australian Battalion to advance on 400 Plateau, at 1500, there was little fighting in the Anzac area on this day.

At both areas the water supply had been considerably improved by the landing of water-tanks supplied from specially designed lighters carrying water from the River Nile.

April 27th.—Submarine E14 passed the Narrows and remained for twenty-two days in the Sea of Marmora.

Offensive operations were postponed at Helles for the capture of Achi Baba, as the whole of the French Brigade promised as a reinforcement could not be landed until late in the day. The 86th Brigade was withdrawn into reserve during the morning, and units were reorganized. A plan to improve the position on the front of the 29th Division was put into operation at 1600 hours. In an hour and a half an advance had been made across the peninsula from the high ground above "S" Beach, where the two French battalions on the right of the 29th Division joined up with the South Wales Borderers, to the mouth of Gully Ravine.

A Turkish transport in the Narrows was sunk by the *Queen Elizabeth*, with the help of the observation of a balloon ship, at a range of 16,500 yards from Gaba Tepe.

At Anzac the 2nd Australian Battalion and the Wellington Battalion succeeded in capturing ground at the head of Walker's Ridge. Touch was finally established between the troops on 400 Plateau, Pope's Hill and Russell's Top. Mustapha Kemel on this day organized an attack on the whole front with sixteen battalions. These attacks were not simultaneous and were easily repulsed. The line (one and a half mile's long) held by the evening of this day ran along Walker's Ridge to the summit of Russell's Top, through the head of Monash

H

Gully to Courtney's on Second Ridge then south-west to the coast through the middle of 400 Plateau. The greatest depth of this position was only a thousand yards from Ari Burnu to Courtney's Post.

April 28th.—Four battalions of Royal Naval Division were dispatched to Anzac. In this area there were twenty battalions opposed to eighteen Turkish battalions.

Turkish reserves were being hurried to the Helles area.

Local attacks were continued by the Turks along the Anzac front. All units in the Anzac Corps had now suffered at least twenty-five per cent casualties.

At Helles the first battle of Krithia was fought. The objectives to be gained on this day were for the French to advance north-east towards, and parallel to, Kereves Dere, keeping their right on Hill 236; the 88th Brigade to continue the line facing east to include Krithia and for the 87th Brigade to join up with the 88th Brigade on Hill 472 and to bring their left flank back to the coast at Sari Tepe, three miles north-east of their present position on the coast near the mouth of Gully Ravine. The troops were tired out with the strain of the last three days' operations.

The difficulty for this operation was that there was little information to give with reference to the enemy, and there were only twenty-eight guns available to support the attack, and artillery ammunition was limited. The Turks now had nine battalions in posts covering the approaches to Krithia from the mouth of the Kereves Dere to " Y " Beach.

The battle started at 0800 hours, supported by the fire from the naval guns and from the artillery. The 86th Brigade and the K.O.S.B. at " W " Beach formed a general reserve.

On some parts of the front of attack there were local successes, and on other parts there were reverses, which caused gaps in the general line. The Turks were being reinforced during the day, our troops were exhausted, the available reserves were used up to reinforce the 88th Brigade in the centre of the line at 1130 hours, and the shortage of artillery ammunition was much felt.

The result of the day's operations was that the Allies' casualties amounted to three thousand and the general line was from a point on the coast three miles north-east of Cape Tekke to the coast half a mile south-west of the mouth of Kereves Dere.

April 29th.—Our line was consolidated. It was realized that unless strong reinforcements were to be available shortly, Kilid Bahr and the Narrows could not be reached.

The Turkish forces on this day were divided into two groups.

THE DARDANELLES CAMPAIGN 99

Essad Pasha commanded the group to oppose the Anzacs. It consisted of the III Corps. The group to oppose the Allies in the Helles area was commanded by von Sodenstern and consisted of the 7th and 9th Turkish Divisions.

Some men were landed by the Navy on the south of Suvla Bay. They went to the top of Lala Baba and destroyed a telephone wire in a trench there.

May 1st.—The 29th Indian Infantry Brigade and two battalions of the Royal Naval Division were landed at Helles. At 2200 hours the Turks made a mass attack against our trenches at Helles in the vicinity of Kirte Dere. At first they were successful in gaining a footing in a part of our trenches. Our reserves drove them out. On the French front the fighting was continued until 0200 hours. A company of the Worcesters on the French left flank and the Howe Battalion on their right helped to defeat the Turks.

At 1000 hours there was an attempt to advance on the whole front of the French and the 29th Divisions. The advances made, however, were uneven, and those parties who got ahead of those on their flanks suffered heavily from enfilade machine-gun and rifle fire. The result was that within an hour the bulk of the attacking force was back to its original positions.

Our losses up to date in killed, wounded and missing now totalled just a few men short of fourteen thousand.

May 2nd.—An attack was made against Baby 700 at 1915 hours by three battalions, namely, the Otago Battalion, and 16th and 13th Australian Battalions after a naval and military bombardment of fifteen minutes. The country was most intricate for night operations to which the troops were unaccustomed. Also, one battalion reached its rendezvous one and a half hour's late, so that there was lack of cohesion and co-operation throughout the attack, which finally broke down under the Turks' infilade fire and counter-attacks.

Fifty men from Anzac were landed in H.M.S. *Colne* near Lala Baba. This party surprised seventeen Turks in a trench on the hill, and took thirteen prisoners. Two escaped and two were killed.

May 3rd.—Further efforts at Anzac were made to capture Baby 700 by reinforcements of two battalions of the Royal Naval Division. The attacks, however, failed. Our casualties were six hundred.

Orders were sent to the Anzac Corps to transfer two brigades to Helles on May 5th and to send five field batteries at once to " W " Beach. These troops, with the 125th Brigade of the 42nd Division, would be available to co-operate in the offensive to be undertaken on May 6th.

Eight Turkish battalions made a night attack against the French line of trenches. They gained a footing in the trenches but later, when they were driven out at dawn, suffered heavy casualties from the French artillery when retreating across the open to their own trenches.

May 4th.—Two battalions of the 2nd Naval Brigade took over 1,100 yards of the front trenches between the telegraph line and the Sedd-el-Bahr—Krithia road from the French Division.

A lighter containing ammunition for 18-pounder guns was accidentally sunk.

The opposing numbers at Helles were now estimated at 25,000 Allied rifles against 20,000 Turkish rifles.

May 5th.—The 125th Brigade arrived at Gully Beach from Helles.

The 2nd Australian Brigade and the New Zealand Brigade were embarked at Anzac Cove. They were taken to "W" Beach and then marched to a reserve position on the right of the line at Helles.

Five Anzac batteries remained at "W" Beach.

On the Anzac front the Turks near Quinn's Post were reported to be carrying out mining operations.

May 6th.—Second battle of Krithia. The final objective for the troops in this battle was the capture of the enemy's main position on Achi Baba.

This was to be carried out by an attack from the west and south-west by the 29th Division, and the troops attached to this division, pivoting on the French troops, whose left flank rested on the Eastern bank of the Kanli Dere.

The French troops were to capture the Kereves Spur and to keep in line with the right of the 29th Division.

This attack was to be supported by six battleships and four cruisers.

Zero was fixed at 1100 hours for the infantry advance. Artillery fire opened at 1030 hours against the located Turkish trenches.

The battle started with the advance of the 88th Brigade. Its progress was checked by the Turks' enfilade fire from both flanks, as on neither side had the troops been able to keep up with them.

By 1600 hours the 88th Brigade consolidated their position on a line four hundred yards from their starting line.

On the left flank there was considerable opposition as soon as our advance was started at 1130 hours, and the expected outflanking movement broke down as no progress could be made against the enemy's accurate and heavy fire. On the

THE DARDANELLES CAMPAIGN

right flank, too, the French were met by heavy fire as soon as they gained the high ground commanding the mouth of the Kereves Dere.

The 2nd Naval Brigade helped the advance of the French left flank towards the Kereves Spur.

By the evening, however, the general results had been disappointing, as the Turks' main position had not been reached. An average advance of four hundred yards had, however, been made.

As our casualties had not been heavy, and as the 127th Brigade were landing during the evening and night, it was decided to continue offensive operations on the following day.

May 7th.—The attack was to be started by the infantry at 1000 hours after a fifteen minutes' bombardment.

The objectives were the same as on the previous day. The 29th Division were not to wait until the French had gained the high ridge above Kereves Dere, but were to push on through Krithia to capture Achi Baba.

The limited ammunition supply made preliminary bombardment and subsequent artillery support ineffective. The enemy's machine guns had not been located by our balloon ship. On the left flank the Turks' machine-gun fire was particularly effective. The 125th Brigade on this flank could make no progress.

The result was that the 88th Brigade on its left could not advance its left flank without being enfiladed. This brigade was also strongly opposed by the Turks on their front at Fir Tree Spur. The result was that they were not able to get farther ahead than three hundred yards from their starting line.

At 1630 hours there was another bombardment on the whole front for fifteen minutes followed by an attack by the 87th and 88th Brigades. Little progress could be made against the Turks' heavy machine-gun fire.

On the right flank the French could make little headway against the strengthened positions along the Kereves Spur. Troops on the left of the French could not advance until their right flank was secure.

The result was that again the Turks' reserves had not been engaged by the end of the day. During the night there was little activity on either side.

May 8th.—The operations were renewed at 1015 hours. There was a bombardment of the Turks' position at this time followed by the advance of the New Zealand Brigade for the capture of Fir Tree Spur. There was no surprise, and the enemy were able to concentrate against this isolated attack.

The result was that though progress was made at first through Fir Tree Wood the New Zealanders were unable to maintain their positions against nine Turkish battalions with whom they were engaged. The Turks had very strong positions on the high ground west of the Kereves ravine. Against these the French troops could make little impression.

An order then was sent from Headquarters for the whole Allied line, reinforced by the Australian line, to fix bayonets and advance on Krithia at 1730 hours.

The fighting was continued until it was dark, when the orders were received by the troops to consolidate the positions which they had reached.

The result of the three days' fighting in the second battle of Krithia was a gain of ground of six hundred yards on the right of the British line and four hundred yards on the left and centre. The Allies' casualties were up to 6,500 in this battle. The Army was now definitely held up by the Turks in such strong and concealed positions that the naval guns could do little to help it to advance.

May 9th.—" From nightfall on May 9th till dawn on May 10th efforts were made everywhere to push us back. Everywhere the assailants were repulsed, and now for the first time I felt that we had planted a fairly firm foothold upon the point of Gallipoli Peninsula." (Despatches.)

The Commander-in-Chief now gave orders for the line held to be strongly fortified and to be divided into sectors, in each of which there would be artillery groups. It was now realized that for the present the attacks should be confined to local actions on sections of the front strongly supported by the available artillery. Every unit had suffered heavily; there were no reserves, ammunition supply was small, and the troops were still three miles from the top of the objective—Achi Baba.

On the Anzac front a raid was carried out from Quinn's Post at 2245 hours.

The Turks were completely surprised and their forward trenches were captured. The Australian troops could not gain contact with each other in the captured trenches and could not in consequence resist the enemy's counter-attacks with grenades. The Australians were finally forced to retire back to their original lines with a loss of two hundred casualties.

May 10th.—The proposal by the naval authorities to attempt to pass the Narrows alone was vetoed. It was necessary for Kilid Bahr to be occupied by the Army before any further attempts were made by the Navy.

May 11th.—The 29th Division was withdrawn from the firing

THE DARDANELLES CAMPAIGN

line. This was the first rest this division had had after eighteen days of almost continuous fighting.

May 12th.—Russian General Headquarters reported that they had had heavy losses in Galicia and in the Carpathians, and that the capitulation of Turkey was most desirable in order to release their army in the Caucasus.

May 14th.—The War Council now considered whether (a) reinforcements to maintain the existing situation should be sent out to Gallipoli; (b) the campaign should be closed; (c) to try to gain a decisive success as suggested by Russian General Headquarters.

Sir Ian Hamilton was accordingly asked to appreciate the situation and to report the numbers he would require to gain his objective.

The second division of the French troops arrived. The French Corps was now commanded by General Gouraud.

May 17th.—Sir Ian Hamilton sent his reply to the War Council to the effect that he would require the assistance of four more divisions unless the Russians would be able to help by sending a Corps to the Bosphorus, or if Greece or Bulgaria co-operated actively, his estimate could be reduced by two divisions.

May 18th.—Lord Kitchener reported that the 52nd Division was about to embark for Gallipoli.

The 2nd Australian Brigade was brought back to Anzac from Helles. The Turks on this front at this time had four divisions.

May 19th.—Before daybreak the Turks attacked in force in the Anzac area against the troops holding 400 Plateau, Quinn's Post, the Nek, Pope's and Courtney's Posts, and on Bolton's Ridge. They were successful only in gaining a footing for a short time in a corner of Courtney's Post. Their successive mass attacks broke down by 0500 hours, and had resulted in no gain of ground and in a loss of some 10,000 casualties. The casualties of our troops were a hundred killed and five hundred wounded.

During the armistice arranged between the opposing forces at Anzac on May 27th some three thousand Turks were buried.

Submarine E11 entered the Sea of Marmora and later sank a Turkish transport near Constantinople.

May 24th.—The three British divisions at Helles were formed into the VIII Corps.

The orders for the troops in this Corps were for a systematic advance of the front-line trenches until they were within assaulting distance of the Turks' forward positions.

May 25th.—A German submarine sank H.M.S. *Triumph* close to Anzac. After this unexpected disaster only one battleship was maintained at Helles and one in the Straits to support the troops and to check the Turks' fire from their battalions on the Asiatic shore.

May 28th.—During the night, on the Anzac front, a Turkish trench on Sazli Beit Dere was captured. This trench was overlooked by Turkish trenches from Table Top. After much fighting the Turks caused the troops holding this trench to vacate it.

May 29th.—A part of the front line near Quinn's Post was blown up in the early morning from a tunnel with which the Turks had undermined the post. The Turks seized the crater and then pressed forward to our second line. The Australians made counter-attacks from the flanks and support trenches and successfully restored the situation by the evening.

May 31st.—The Commander-in-Chief decided to carry out a general action at Helles on June 4th. It was now estimated that the Turks had over eighty thousand men in the vicinity of the Gallipoli Peninsula.

The Commander-in-Chief therefore decided that the first objectives were to be the enemy's front-line system of trenches.

June 4th.—The third battle of Krithia. The Turkish 9th Division was on their right front holding positions on Gully Spur and Fir Tree Spur; their 12th Division was on their left front holding positions on Krithia Spur and Kereves Spur. In reserve the Turks had three divisions. Their total strength was approximately 28,000 rifles and 86 guns and howitzers. On our front the 29th Indian Infantry Brigade were holding positions on Gully Spur; the 88th Brigade were holding Fir Tree Spur; the 127th Brigade held positions on Krithia Spur up to Kanli Dere; the 2nd Naval Brigade held between Kanli Dere to the telegraph line running south-west to Sedd-el-Bahr, and the French troops continued the line on the Kereves Spur to the coast. The Allies were approximately 30,000 strong.

After an intensive bombardment for half an hour the Allies left their trenches and started the assault.

On the French front there were heavy casualties as soon as the advance started.

A footing was gained in the Haricot redoubt, but the position gained could not be maintained for long.

The 2nd Naval Brigade, on the front of the Royal Naval Division, at first were able to make progress, but when their right flank was enfiladed by the Turks from the high ground on Kereves Spur they suffered so heavily that they were forced to withdraw to their original position.

On the front of the 42nd Division the 127th Brigade made a splendid advance to a depth of approximately a thousand yards, especially on the right of their line.

The 88th Brigade, on the left of the Naval Brigade, suffered heavily from machine-gun posts, which had not been damaged by our artillery fire; but in spite of losses were able to secure the greater part of their first objective.

On the left of the line little progress could be made as the Turkish trenches in the vicinity of Gully Ravine had been very little damaged, and there was little artillery available to support the advance of the troops.

Two hours after zero the situation was that an advance had been made in the centre only, but the French and British corps reserves were intact.

The Corps Commanders decided to use their reserves in gaining ground where the troops had been checked, and where the Turks were strong and with high morale, and not in exploiting success.

The result was that three hours' later the bulk of the reserves were used up without appreciable gain of ground anywhere.

The Turks were reinforced during the afternoon. At 1800 hours the 127th Brigade was heavily attacked from three sides and forced to retire.

The result of the day's fighting on the front of 5,000 yards was a gain of ground of 250 yards in some places, and up to 500 yards in others, and the capture of two lines of enemy trenches on a front of a mile between Kanli Dere and Gully Ravine. Our casualties were 4,500 and the French lost 2,000.

During the night the ground gained was consolidated in spite of the Turks' counter-attacks.

Our losses since the landing were now nearly 39,000.

June 6th.—The Turks tried to recapture some trenches in the Kirte Dere half a mile north-east of Fir Tree Wood. The Turks regained one line of trenches, but were unable to recapture a strong second line which the 88th Brigade had constructed.

The Commander-in-Chief cabled to Lord Kitchener: "I believe the reinforcements asked for in my telegram of May 17th will eventually enable me to take Kilid Bahr and will assuredly expedite the decision."

CHAPTER XV.

June 7th to end of the Campaign.

June 7th.—There was a meeting of the Dardanelles Committee to discuss whether (*a*) the Gallipoli Campaign was to be abandoned or not; (*b*) sufficient reinforcements should be sent to the Ægean to enable the Commander-in-Chief to undertake an immediate offensive; (*c*) gradual advance should be attempted with the troops available.

Lord Kitchener favoured the plan of continuing the offensive. The Committee then decided to send out three divisions of the First New Army and to strengthen the fleet.

June 8th.—The Commander-in-Chief agreed to reinforce the Anzac Corps with one of the three new divisions promised to him. Later it was decided that two of these three divisions should be sent to the Anzac Corps for the capture of Chunuk Bair, and that additional divisions should be used farther north.

June 10th.—During the night of June 10th/11th the 1st Border Regiment and the 2nd South Wales Borderers made a raid to capture the Turkish posts called " Boomerang " and " Turkey Trench " on the eastern side of the Gully Ravine. The Border Regiment captured and retained seventy yards of " Turkey Trench." The " Boomerang " trench could not be held against the Turks' repeated counter-attacks.

June 13th.—On the night of June 15th/16th the Turks made a determined attack on the trench gained by the Border Regiment in " Turkey Trench." They were able to recapture their lost ground during the night. At 0500 hours a detachment of the 1st Royal Munster Fusiliers regained the trench after a determined bombing attack.

June 21st.—The French carried out an attack on a 650 yards front with the object of seizing the crest of Kereves Spur. This attack was carried out by the 6th Colonial Regiment on the right and the 176th Regiment on the left. The French troops were opposed by the Turkish 2nd Division immediately on their front.

The infantry assault started at 0600 hours after an artillery bombardment of three-quarters of an hour.

At first the assault was successful against the enemy's front line trenches, except on the extreme left, where the Turks were able to hold a strong redoubt called the Quadrilateral. On the right the Turks' trenches, when occupied, were found

THE DARDANELLES CAMPAIGN

to be so much destroyed by the original bombardment that there was little cover available.

The 6th Colonial Regiment, on the right, were unable to remain in their captured trenches, and withdrew to their own positions.

The attack was renewed at midday without success.

At 1845 hours a fresh regiment was brought up to carry out the attack and join up with the positions being held by the 176th Regiment. This was successfully accomplished.

June 23rd.—The French tried to improve their positions on the crest of the Kereves Spur. They gained a little ground in the centre of their position, but were unable to capture the Quadrilateral. Their casualties had been 2,500. The Turks lost over 6,000.

June 28th.—An attack was made against the Turkish defences, consisting of five lines of trenches on Gully Spur, and also two lines of trenches on a 700 yards front on Fir Tree Spur. On this front the Turks had two divisions covered by approximately seventy guns and howitzers.

Our attacking troops were the 29th Division, the 29th Indian Infantry Brigade, and the 156th Brigade of the 52nd Division, supported by a cruiser and two destroyers and seventy-seven guns and howitzers.

The bombardment started at 0900 hours until 1045 hours, when the Border Regiment rushed forward and captured Boomerang Redoubt. On Gully Spur the 87th Brigade captured their objectives easily.

East of Gully Ravine progress was not easy as the artillery bombardment, through lack of high explosives, had not been effective.

Our losses were heavy. The Turks made many bombing counter-attacks, which our troops had great difficulty in withstanding, as there was a shortage of effective bombs. Our left flank faced east instead of north-east, and was within a mile of Krithia. There were no reserves available to exploit this success, and on the right flank heavy fighting continued in order to maintain the position there as the original assault had not been successful.

June 28th.—A demonstration was made at Anzac from Tasman Post. Enemy's positions on the lower spurs of Pine Ridge were occupied. The Turks brought up reinforcements from Eski Keui.

These troops were heavily shelled by our artillery and from our destroyers. During the evening our troops withdrew to the Tasman Post trenches.

June 29th.—The Turks attacked strongly after midnight at

Anzac against our line at Quinn's Post, Pope's Hill and Russell Top. They were successful in gaining a footing into our trenches at some points, but they were driven out before daylight and suffered heavily.

The Turks made many counter-attacks against the 87th and 88th Brigades consolidating the captured grounds. The position was maintained.

June 30th.—The 7th French Colonial Regiment captured and retained part of the Quadrilateral.

The Turks made a determined attack against our left flank from the Nullah against positions held by the 1st/5th and 1st/6th Gurkhas. The Turks were successful at first, but later were driven out of the trenches they had captured by a counter-attack of the Gurkhas armed with kukris.

July 1st.—The Turks made a bombing attack on the positions held by the 2nd/10th Gurkhas and by the Royal Inniskilling Fusiliers. They succeeded in gaining a footing in our trenches owing to their superiority in bombs. Later they were driven out by the counter-attacks of the Royal Inniskilling Fusiliers. The regained trench was later vacated by our troops, who withdrew, owing to a misunderstanding, to a barricade erected farther back. The Turks then reoccupied the trench without opposition.

July 5th.—The Turks at Krithia made an unsuccessful dawn attack on the French and British trenches. They suffered heavily in their attempt to reach our positions.

July 12th.—At 0735 hours the Turks' trenches at Helles were attacked after a preliminary bombardment. The French Corps attacked on the right flank, and the 52nd Division on the right centre on a 3,000 yards front from the mouth of the Kereves Dere to the Sedd-el-Bahr—Krithia road. The 29th Division attacked west of this road.

An advance was made on the front of the French Corps and of the 52nd Division.

July 13th.—Our attacks at Helles were renewed at 1630 hours. During the two days' fighting an advance of two hundred to four hundred yards on different parts of the front was made at a cost of three thousand casualties.

The Turks casualties were estimated at five thousand, and five hundred prisoners were taken.

August 6th.—At 1530 hours the 88th Brigade at Helles attacked the Turkish trenches on a mile of front across the two forks of the Kirte Dere. The Turks were in great strength in this area, and as there was inadequate support the attack failed with a loss of nearly 2,000 men to the 88th Brigade.

THE DARDANELLES CAMPAIGN

The further attacks ordered for the 86th Brigade during the night were cancelled.

Operations started at 1630 hours at Anzac, with an attack by the 1st Australian Brigade against the enemy's position on Lone Pine. In spite of the strength of the Turks' trenches with overhead cover and of heavy losses in the assault the attack was successful.

The Turks counter-attacked, but the Australians were reinforced and maintained their positions, and also drew towards the captured trenches available Turkish reserves.

At Suvla covering troops were landed, namely, three infantry brigades of the 11th Division, at 2230 hours. The hills round Suvla Bay were then to be seized. It was hoped that at dawn Chocolate Hill and Ismail Oglu Tepe and the high ground north and east of Suvla Bay would be taken. The remainder of the force was to push on to the Anafarta Hills.

The 32nd and 33rd Brigades landed at "B" and "C" Beaches.

The 34th Brigade landed at "A" Beach. Lala Baba was captured by two battalions of the 32nd Brigade, which had disembarked at "B" Beach.

The 34th Brigade was checked by the enemy on Hill 10. The 32nd Brigade was sent to help in the capture of this hill, from which the enemy were finally driven.

A footing was also gained on Karakol Dagh.

During the morning six battalions of the 10th Division were landed. Three more battalions of the 10th Division arrived later at "C" Beach.

August 7th.—The 42nd Division attacked the Turkish lines at 0940 hours on a front of 800 yards south of the position previously attacked by the 88th Brigade. On the front of the 125th Brigade a portion of the Turks' second line was captured, and later incorporated in the main British position. Casualties in the two attacking brigades, however, were heavy.

It was decided, therefore, to hold the existing positions at Helles until the offensive operations at Suvla and Anzac had caused the Turks to withdraw some of their force from the Helles area.

The objectives at Anzac on this day were first to capture the enemy posts guarding the lower reaches of Chailak Dere and Sazli Beit Dere. Then at 2245 hours the two assaulting columns were to secure Chunuk Bair and Hill 971. The Australian Light Horse were to capture the Nek and Baby 700 at dawn; assisted by subsidiary attacks made on the Turkish trenches opposite Quinn's Post and Pope's Hill.

By 0600 hours the assaulting columns had not reached their

objectives, and the dawn attacks had failed. Turkish reinforcements were being hurried forward to vulnerable points. Two regiments reached the main ridge from Chunuk Bair to Hill 971 soon after 0700 hours. The 7th and 12th Turkish Divisions were ordered to march south from Bulair, and the 8th Division from Helles was sent to Anzac.

At Suvla ground was gained east of the Salt Lake from Karakol Dagh to Chocolate Hill. The objectives, however, were still in the Turks' possession.

The Turks in this area had three battalions, as opposed to twenty-two battalions of the IX Corps, which were ashore. Our losses had amounted to approximately 1,700 men.

The Turkish troops were disposed as follows:—Opposite our three battalions on Kiretch Tepe Sirt were three Gendarmenè companes. On the western edge of the Anafarta Sagir Spur there were 300 men. On the Ismail Oglu Tepe Spur were 800 men and five machine guns. They had one battery on Kavak Tepe and one battery on Tekka Tepe.

August 8th.—The Turks withdrew their artillery from the forward positions at Suvla in order to avoid capture. At 1130 hours the IX Corps Commander ordered his divisions to advance with the qualification that "in view of adequate artillery support an attack on an entrenched position held in strength" was not to be carried out.

The result was that nothing was accomplished at Suvla on this day.

The inaction of the troops at Suvla caused the Commander-in-Chief to make a visit to this area. He urged the Commander of the 11th Division to make an early advance in order to forestall the enemy, who were known to be bringing up reinforcements.

The 32nd Brigade accordingly was ordered to advance on to the high ground north of Anafarta Sagir to Kavak Tepe by dawn on August 9th before Turkish reinforcements could arrive there.

Mustafa Kemal directed two battalions of the 12th Division respectively towards Kavak Tepe and Tekke Tepe.

It was estimated that the Turks would now have twelve battalions and thirty guns to oppose the IX Corps.

Sir Ian Hamilton has described the situation on August 8th as follows in his Despatches dated 11th December, 1915:—

"And now General Stopford, recollecting the vast issues which hung upon his success in forestalling the enemy, urged his Divisional commanders to push on. Otherwise, as he saw, all the advantages of the surprise landing must be nullified. But the Divisional Commanders believed themselves, it seems, to be unable to move. Their men, they said, were exhausted by their efforts of the night of the 6th-7th and by the action of the 7th. The want of water had told on the new troops. The distribution from the beaches had not worked smoothly. In some cases the hose had been pierced by individuals wishing to fill their own bottles; in others, lighters had grounded so far from the beach that men swam out to fill batches of water-bottles. All this had added to the disorganization inevitable after a night landing, followed by fights here and there with an enemy scattered over a country to us unknown. These pleas for delay were perfectly well founded. But it seems to have been overlooked that the half-defeated Turks in front of us were equally exhausted and disorganized, and that an advance was the simplest and swiftest method of solving the water trouble and every other sort of trouble. Be this as it may, the objections overbore the Corps Commander's resolution. He had now got ashore three batteries (two of them mountain batteries), and the great guns of the ships were ready to speak at his request. But it was lack of artillery support which finally decided him to acquiesce in a policy of going slow which, by the time it reached the troops, became translated into a period of inaction. The Divisional Generals were, in fact, informed that, "in view of the inadequate artillery support," General Stopford did not wish them to make frontal attacks on entrenched positions, but desired them, so far as was possible, to try and turn any trenches which were met with. Within the terms of this instruction lies the root of our failure to make use of the priceless daylight hours of August 8th.

"Normally, it may be correct to say that in modern warfare infantry cannot be expected to advance without artillery preparation. But in a landing on a hostile shore the order has to be inverted. The infantry must advance and seize a suitable position to cover the landing, and to provide artillery positions for the main thrust. The very existence of the force, its water supply, its facilities for munitions and supplies, its power to reinforce, must absolutely depend on the infantry being able instantly to make good sufficient ground without the aid of the artillery other than can be supplied for the purpose by *floating* batteries.

"This is not a condition that should take the commander of a covering force by surprise. It is one already foreseen. Driving power was required, and even a certain ruthlessness, to brush aside pleas for a respite for tired troops. The one fatal error was inertia. And inertia prevailed.

"Late in the evening of the 7th the enemy had withdrawn the few guns which had been in action during the day. Beyond half a dozen shells dropped from very long range into the bay in the early morning of the 8th, no enemy artillery fired that day in the Suvla area. The guns had evidently been moved back, lest they should be captured when we pushed forward. As for the entrenched positions, these, in the ordinary acceptance of the term, were non-existent. The General Staff Officer whom I had sent on to Suvla early in the morning of the 8th reported by telegraph the absence of hostile gun-fire, the small amount of rifle fire, and the enemy's apparent weakness. He also drew attention to the inaction of our own troops, and to the fact that golden opportunities were being missed. Before this message arrived at General Headquarters I had made up my mind, from the Corps Commander's own reports, that all was not well at Suvla. There was risk in cutting myself adrift, even temporarily, from touch with the operations at Anzac and Helles; but I did by best to provide against any sudden call by leaving Major-General W. P. Braithwaite, my Chief of the General Staff, in charge, with instructions to keep me closely informed of events at the other two fronts; and, having done this, I took ship and set out for Suvla.

"On arrival at about 5 p.m. I boarded H.M.S. *Jonquil*, where I found corps headquarters, and where General Stopford informed be that the General Officer Commanding 11th Division was confident of success in an attack he was to make at dawn next morning (the 9th). I felt no such confidence. Beyond a small advance by a part of the 11th Division between the Chocolate Hills and Ismail Oglu Tepe, and some further progress along the Kiretch Tepe Sirt ridge by the 10th Division, the day of the 8th had been lost. The Commander of the 11th Division had, it seems, ordered strong patrols to be pushed forward so as to make good all the strong positions in advance which could be occupied without serious fighting; but, as he afterwards reported, " little was done in this respect." Thus a priceless twelve hours had already gone to help the chances of the Turkish reinforcements which were, I knew, both from naval and aerial sources, actually on the march for Suvla. But when I urged that even now, at the eleventh hour, the 11th Division should make a concerted attack upon the hills, I was met by a *non possumus*. The objections of the morning were no longer valid; the men were now well rested, watered, and fed. But the Divisional Commanders disliked the idea of an advance by night, and General Stopford did not care, it seemed, to force their hands.

"So it came about that I was driven to see whether I could

THE DARDANELLES CAMPAIGN 113

not, myself, put concentration of effort and purpose into the direction of the large number of men ashore. The Corps Commander made no objection. He declared himself to be as eager as I could be to advance. The representations made by the Divisional Commanders had seemed to him insuperable. If I could see my way to get over them no one would be more pleased than himself.

" I landed on the beach, where all seemed quiet and peaceful, and saw the Commander of the 11th Division. I warned him the sands were running out fast, and that by dawn the high ground to his front might very likely be occupied in force by the enemy. He saw the danger, but declared that it was a physical impossibility, at so late an hour (6 p.m.), to get out orders for a night attack, the troops being very much scattered. There was no other difficulty now, but this was insuperable; he could not recast his orders or get them round to his troops in time. But one Brigade, the 32nd, was more or less concentrated and ready to move. I, therefore, issued a direct order that, even if it were only the 32nd Brigade, the advance should begin at the earliest possible moment, so that a portion at least of the 11th Division should anticipate the Turkish reinforcements on the heights and dig themselves in there upon some good tactical point.

"In taking upon myself the serious responsibility of thus dealing with a detail of divisional tactics I was careful to limit the scope of the interference. Beyond directing that the one brigade which was reported ready to move at once should try and make good the heights before the enemy got on to them I did nothing, and said not a word calculated to modify or in any way affect the attack already planned for the morning. Out of the thirteen battalions which were to have advanced against the heights at dawn, four were now to anticipate that movement by trying to make good the key of the enemy's position at once and under cover of darkness.

" In General Stopford's despatch he says that, " One company of the 6th East Yorks Pioneer Battalion succeeded in getting to the top of the hill north of Anafarta Sagir, but the rest of the battalion and the 32nd Brigade were attacked from both flanks during their advance, and fell back to a line north and south of Sulajik. Very few of the leading company or the Royal Engineers who accompanied it got back, and that evening the strength of the battalion was nine officers and 380 men."

" After their retirement from the hill north of Anafarta Sagir (which commanded the whole battlefield) this 32nd Brigade then still marked the high-water level of the advance made at dawn by the rest of the division. When their first retirement was completed they had to fall back farther, so as to come into line with the most forward of their comrades. The inference seems clear. Just as the 32nd Brigade in their advance met with markedly less opposition than the troops who attacked an hour and a half later, so, had they themselves started earlier, they would probably have experienced less opposition. Further, it seems reasonable to suppose that had the complete division started at 4 a.m. on the 9th, or, better still, at 10 p.m. on the 8th, they would have made good the whole of the heights in front of them.

"That night I stayed at Suvla, preferring to drop direct cable contact with my operations as a whole to losing touch with a corps battle which seemed to be going wrong.

"At dawn on the 9th I very soon realized, by the well sustained artillery fire of the enemy (so silent the previous day), and by the volume of the musketry, that Turkish reinforcements had arrived; that with the renewed confidence caused by our long delay the guns had been brought back; and that, after all, we were forestalled. This was a bad moment. Our attack failed; our losses were very serious. The enemy's enfilading shrapnel fire seemed to be especially destructive and demoralizing, the shell bursting low and all along our line. Time after time it threw back our attack just as it seemed upon the point of making good. The 33rd Brigade at first made most hopeful progress in its attempt to seize Ismail Oglu Tepe. Some of the leading troops gained the summit, and were able to look over on the other side. Many Turks were killed there. Then the centre seemed to give way. Whether this was the result of the shrapnel fire or whether, as some say, an order to retire came up from the rear, the result was equally fatal to success. Scrub fires on Hill 70 did much to harass and hamper our troops. When the 32nd Brigade fell back before attacks from the slopes of the hill north of Anafarta Sagir and from the direction of Abrijka they took up the line north and south through Sulajik. Here their left was protected by two battalions of the 34th Brigade, which came up to their support. The line was later on prolonged by the remainder of the 34th Brigade and two battalions of the 159th Brigade of the 53rd Division. Their right was connected with the Chocolate Hills by the 33rd Brigade on the position to which they had returned after their repulse from the upper slopes of Ismail Oglu Tepe."

August 9th.—The 53rd Division, less artillery, were landed at Suvla. The troops of this division were scattered over the front, reinforcing the 11th Division.

THE DARDANELLES CAMPAIGN

The 32nd Brigade, on arrival at Tekke Tepe, found that the Turks were holding this spur in strength, and were unable to capture it.

The result of the day's fighting was that the 11th Division withdrew back to its original position after having suffered heavy losses.

August 10th.—The 53rd Division attacked the Turks holding positions on the Anafarta Hills, supported by the 11th Division and by the 59th Field Brigade, R.A., two Highland mountain batteries and the guns of warships.

The result was that, as the Turks were not surprised and had strengthened their positions, the 53rd Division, after some gain of ground at the outset, was finally obliged to fall back to a general line running from the Azmak Dere through Green Hill and West of Kuchuk Anafarta Ova to the position held by the 10th Division on the Kiretch Tepe Sirt.

Sir Ian Hamilton described the fighting at Anzac on August 10th as follows, in his despatches dated December 11th, 1915:—

" At daybreak on Tuesday, August 10th, the Turks delivered a grand attack from the line Chunuk Bair-Hill Q against these two battalions, already weakened in numbers, though not in spirit by previous fighting. First our men were shelled by every enemy gun, and then, at 5.30 a.m., were assaulted by a huge column, consisting of no less than a full division plus a regiment of three battalions. The ponderous mass of the enemy swept over the crest, turned the right flank of our line below, swarmed round the Hampshires and General Baldwin's column, which had to give ground, and were only extricated with great difficulty and very heavy losses.

" Now it was our turn. The warships and the New Zealand and Australian Artillery, the Indian Mountain Artillery Brigade, and the 69th Brigade Royal Field Artillery were getting the chance of a lifetime. As the successive solid lines of Turks topped the crest of the ridge gaps were torn through their formation, and an iron rain fell on them as they tried to re-form in the gullies.

" Not here only did the Turks pay dearly for their recapture of the vital crest. Enemy reinforcements continued to move up Battleship Hill under heavy and accurate fire from our guns, and still they kept topping the ridges and pouring down the western slopes of the Chunuk Bair as if determined to regain everything they had lost. But once they were over the crest they became exposed not only to the full blast of the guns, naval and military, but also to a battery of ten machine guns belonging to the New Zealand Infantry Brigade, which played upon their serried ranks at close range until the barrels were red hot. Enormous losses were inflicted, especially by these ten machine-guns; and, of the swarms which had once fairly crossed the crest line, only the merest handful ever straggled back to their own side of Chunuk Bair.

"At the same time strong forces of the enemy (forces which I had reckoned would have been held back to meet our advance from Sulva Bay) were hurled against the Farm and the spurs to the north-east, where there arose a conflict so deadly that it may be considered as the climax of the four days' fighting for the ridge. Portions of our line were pierced, and the troops driven clean down the hill. Generals fought in the ranks and men dropped their scientific weapons and caught one another by the throat. So desperate a battle cannot be described. The Turks came on again and again, fighting magnificently, calling upon the name of God. Our men stood to it, and maintained, by many a deed of daring, the old traditions of their race.

"Towards this supreme struggle the absolute last two battalions from the General Reserve were now hurried, but by 10 a.m. the effort of the enemy was spent. Soon their shattered remnants began to trickle back, leaving a track of corpses behind them, and by night, except prisoners or wounded, no live Turk was left upon our side of the slope.

"That same day, August 10th, two attacks, one in the morning and the other in the afternoon, were delivered on our positions along the Asmak Dere and Damakjelik Bair. Both were repulsed with heavy losses by the 4th Australian Brigade and the 4th South Wales Borderers, the men of the New Army showing all the steadiness of veterans.

"By evening the total casualties of General Birdwood's force had reached 12,000, and included a very large proportion of officers. But physically, though Birdwood's forces were prepared to hold all they had got, they were now too exhausted to attack—at least until they had rested and reorganized. So far they *had* held on to all they had gained, excepting only the footholds on the ridge between Chunuk Bair and Hill Q, momentarily carried by the Gurkhas, and the salient of Chunuk Bair itself, which they had retained for forty-eight hours. Unfortunately, these two pieces of ground, small and worthless as they seemed, were worth, according to the ethics of war, 10,000 lives, for by their loss or retention they just marked the difference between an important success and a signal victory.

"The grand coup had not come off. The Narrows were still out of sight and beyond field gun range."

THE DARDANELLES CAMPAIGN

August 11th.—The infantry of the 54th Division were landed at Suvla. It was decided that this division should make a night march and dawn attack on August 13th against the Turks' positions at Kavak Tepe and Tekke Tepe. This plan was later abandoned.

August 12th.—The 163rd Brigade endeavoured, without success, to clear the Turks from the intersected ground north of Sulajik.

August 15th.—The 30th and 31st Brigades attacked along the top of the Kiretch Tepe Sirt Ridge, supported on their right in the low ground by the 162nd Brigade.

The result of the day's fighting was that the left flank of the 10th Division was considerably advanced.

General de Lisle took command temporarily of the IX Corps.

August 16th.—The Turks' counter-attacked with bombs against the positions gained on Kiretch Tepe Sirt on the previous day.

The 10th Division was forced back to their original line.

August 21st.—The troops at Suvla attacked the Turks' positions on Scimitar Hill and Ismail Oglu Tepe. In spite of heavy losses there was an appreciable advance at first. Eventually it was necessary to fall back to the original positions.

On the Anzac front General Cox's force, consisting of the 29th Indian Brigade, the New Zealand Mounted Rifles, and units from the 10th and 13th Divisions, advanced towards Hill 60. The positions gained by this force made it possible during the next few days to join the left of the Anzac front to the right flank of the troops on the Suvla front north of Azmak Dere. A well at Kabak Kuyu was captured on this day.

August 27th.—A composite force under General Cox started operations, which in the course of two days enabled them to capture Hill 60. A continuous line of trench was now linked up between a point near to Gaba Tepe to Kiretch Tepe Sirt.

General the Hon. J. H. Byng took command of the IX Corps.

September 25th.—The Commander-in-Chief was informed that two British divisions and probably one French division must be taken for service at Salonika.

October 11th.—The Commander-in-Chief was asked for his views as to evacuation.

His reply was that such a step would be wrong both politically and strategically.

October 16th.—Sir Ian Hamilton received orders to return to England.

October 28th.—General Sir Charles Monro arrived at Imbros to command the forces at Gallipoli and the 10th Division and the British detachments already sent to Salonika.

November 3rd.—In his despatches, dated March 6th, 1916, General Monro describes the situation on the Peninsula as follows:—

"The troops on the Peninsula had suffered much from various causes.

"(a) It was not in the first place possible to withdraw them from the shell-swept area as is done when necessary in France, for every corner on the Peninsula is exposed to hostile fire.

"(b) They were much enervated from the diseases which are endemic in that part of Europe in the summer.

"(c) In consequence of the losses which they had suffered in earlier battles, there was a very grave dearth of officers competent to take command of men.

"(d) In order to maintain the numbers needed to hold the front, the Territorial Divisions had been augmented by the attachment of Yeomanry and Mounted Brigades. Makeshifts of this nature very obviously did not tend to create efficiency."

General Monro telegraphed to the War Office that there was no military advantage in our continuing to occupy the Peninsula. His summary of the situation in his despatches was as follows:—

"(a) It was obvious that the Turks could hold us in front with a small force, and prosecute their designs on Baghdad or Egypt or both.

"(b) An advance from the positions we held could not be regarded as a reasonable military operation to expect.

"(c) Even had we been able to make an advance in the Peninsula, our position would not have been ameliorated to any marked degree, and an advance on Constantinople was quite out of the question.

"(d) Since we could not hope to achieve any purpose by remaining on the Peninsula, the appalling cost to the nation involved in consequence of embarking an overseas expedition, with no base available for the rapid transit of stores, supplies and personnel, made it urgent that we should divert the troops locked up on the Peninsula to a more useful theatre."

November 21st.—A violent storm started, followed by twelve hours' rain without intermission. Then there was a blizzard for three days.

THE DARDANELLES CAMPAIGN

In this connection General Monro, in his despatches, writes as follows:—

"On November 21st the Peninsula was visited by a storm said to be nearly unprecedented for the time of the year. The storm was accompanied by torrential rain, which lasted for twenty-four hours. This was followed by hard frost and a heavy blizzard. In the areas of the 8th Corps and the Anzac Corps the effects were not felt to a very marked degree owing to the protection offered by the surrounding hills. The 9th Corps were less favourably situated; the water courses in this area became converted into surging rivers, which carried all before them. The water rose in many places to the height of the parapets, and all means of communications were prevented. The men, drenched as they were by the rain, suffered from the subsequent blizzard most severely. Large numbers collapsed from exposure and exhaustion, and in spite of untiring efforts that were made to mitigate the suffering, I regret to announce that there were 200 deaths from exposure and over 10,000 sick evacuated during the first few days of December.

"From reports given by deserters it is probable that the Turks suffered even to a greater degree.

"In this period our flimsy piers, breakwaters and light shipping became damaged by the storm to a degree which might have involved most serious consequences, and was a very potent indication of the dangers attached to the maintenance and supply of an army operating on a coast line with no harbour, and devoid of all the accessories, such as wharves, piers, cranes and derricks for the discharge and distribution of stores, etc."

December 8th.—Orders were sent to the Commander-in-Chief to withdraw his forces from Anzac and Suvla. The troops at Helles were to be left in that area for the present.

In his despatches, dated March 6th, 1916, General Monro described the general principles on which the evacuation should be undertaken as follows:—

"An evacuation could best be conducted by subdivision into three stages.

"The first, during which all troops, animals and supplies not required for defence during a period when the conditions of weather might retard the evacuation, or, in fact, seriously alter the programme contemplated. The third or final stage, in which the troops on shore should be embarked with all possible speed, leaving behind such guns, animals and stores as were needed for military reasons at this period.

"The problem with which we were confronted was the

withdrawal of an army of a considerable size from positions in no case more than 300 yards from the enemy's trenches, and its embarkation on open beaches, every part of which was within range of Turkish guns, and from which, in winds from the south and south-west, the withdrawal of troops was not possible.

"The attitude which we should adopt, from a naval and military point of view, in case of a withdrawal from the Peninsula being ordered, had given me much anxious thought. According to text-book principles and lessons from history, it seemed essential that this operation of evacuation should be immediately preceded by a combined naval and military feint in the neighbourhood of the Peninsula, with a view to distracting the attention of the Turks from our intention. When endeavouring to work out the concrete fact how such principles could be applied to the situation of our forces, I came to the conclusion that our chances of success were infinitely more probable if we made no departure of any kind from the normal life, which we were following both on sea and land. A feint which did not fulfil its purpose would have been worse than useless, and there was obvious danger that the suspicion of the Turks would be aroused by our adoption of a course, the real purport of which would not have been long disguised."

December 17th.—By this date all troops, animals and supplies not required for the actual conduct of operations were withdrawn.

December 18th.—During the night December 18th/19th approximately 11,000 men and the guns and stores not required in the final stage of evacuation were embarked.

December 19th.—During the night of December 19th/20th the remaining troops, approximately 11,000, guns and stores were embarked. "The evacuation of the Ari Burnu and Anafarta fronts will stand before the eyes of all strategists of retreat as a hitherto quite unattained masterpiece."*

General Monro describes the final phase of the evacuation in his despatches as follows:—

"The good fortune which had attended the evacuation continued during the night of the 19th/20th. The night was perfectly calm, with a slight haze over the moon, an additional stroke of good luck, as there was a full moon on that night.

"Soon after dark the covering ships were all in position, and the final withdrawal began. At 1.30 a.m. the withdrawal

---

* *vide* The Dardanelles Campaign. N. W. Nevinson.

THE DARDANELLES CAMPAIGN

of the rear parties commenced from the front trenches at Suvla and the left of Anzac. Those on the right of Anzac who were nearer the beach remained in position until 2 a.m. By 5.30 a.m. the last man had quitted the trenches.

"At Anzac, four eighteen-pounder guns, two five-inch howitzers, one 4.7 naval gun, one anti-aircraft, and two three-pounder Hotchkiss guns were left, but they were destroyed before the troops finally embarked. In addition, fifty-six mules, a certain number of carts, mostly stripped of their wheels, and some supplies, which were set on fire, were also abandoned.

"At Suvla every gun, vehicle and animal was embarked, and all that remained was a small stock of supplies, which were burnt."

1916.

December 28th.—Orders were received for the Helles area to be evacuated with 40,000 men, 4,500 animals and 150 guns.

January 1st.—The French infantry at Helles were relieved during the night January 1st/2nd.

General Monro, in his despatches, dated March 6th, 1916, describes the state of affairs as follows:—

"The situation on the Peninsula had not materially changed owing to our withdrawal from Suvla and Anzac, except that there was a markedly increased activity in aerial activity over our positions and the islands of Mudros and Imbros, and that hostile patrolling of our trenches was more frequent and more daring. The most important factor was that the number of heavy guns on the European and Asiatic shores had been considerably augmented, and that these guns were liberally supplied with German ammunition, the result of which was that our beaches were being continually shelled, especially from the Asiatic shore. I gave it as my opinion that in my judgment I did not regard a feint as an operation offering any prospect of success. Time, the uncertainty of the weather conditions in the Ægean, the absence of a suitable locality, and the withdrawal of small craft from the main issue for such an operation, were some of the reason which influenced me in the decision at which I aimed.

"With the concurrence of the Vice-Admiral, therefore, it was decided that the navy should do their utmost to pursue a course of retaliation against the Turkish batteries, but to refrain from any unusually aggressive attitude should the Turkish guns remain quiescent."

January 7th.—The 12th Turkish Division attacked our 13th Division on the left of the line at Helles.

THE DARDANELLES CAMPAIGN

General Monro describes the action on this day in his despatches dated March 6th, 1916:—

"On January 7th the enemy developed heavy artillery fire on the trenches held by the 13th Division, while the Asiatic guns shelled those occupied by the Royal Naval Division. The bombardment, which was reported to be the heaviest experienced since we landed in April, lasted from noon till 5 p.m., and was intensive between 3 p.m. and 3.30. Considerable damage was done to our parapets and communication trenches, and telephone communications were interrupted. At 3.30 p.m. two Turkish mines were sprung near Fusilier Bluff, and the Turkish trenches were seen to be full of men whom their officers appeared to be urging to the assault. No attack, however, was developed, except against Fusilier Bluff, where a half-hearted assault was quickly repulsed. Our shortage of artillery at this time was amply compensated for by the support received from fire of the supporting squadron."

During the night January 7th/8th embarkation was successfully carried out, leaving only the troops to be embarked in accordance with the plan. By this time rather more than half the troops had left the Peninsula.

January 8th.—The last troops on the Peninsula were embarked at "W" Beach at 0330 hours on the night of January 8th/9th.

It was not until the stores on the beach were set on fire that the Turks realized that once more the British troops on their front had embarked during the night.

General Monro, in his despatches dated March 6th, 1916, gives the following account of the phase of the evacuation:—

"At 3.30 a.m. the evacuation was complete, and abandoned heaps of stores and supplies were successfully set on fire by time fuzes after the last man had embarked. Two magazines of ammunition and explosives were also successfully blown up at 4 a.m. These conflagrations were apparently the first intimation received by the Turks that we had withdrawn. Red lights were immediately discharged from the enemy's trenches, and heavy artillery fire opened on our trenches and beaches. This shelling was maintained until about 6.30 a.m.

"Apart from four unserviceable fifteen-pounders which had been destroyed earlier in the month, ten worn-out fifteen-pounders, one six-inch Mark VII gun, and six old heavy French guns, all of which were previously blown up, were left on the Peninsula. In addition to the above, 508 animals, most

THE DARDANELLES CAMPAIGN

of which were destroyed, and a number of vehicles and considerable quantities of stores, material, and supplies, all of which were destroyed by burning, had to be abandoned.

"It would have been possible, of course, by extending the period during which the process of evacuation proceeded to have reduced the quantity of stores and material that was left behind on the Peninsula, but not to the degree that may seem apparent at first sight. Our chances of enjoying a continuity of fine weather in the Ægean were very slender in the month of January; it was, indeed, a contingency that had to be reckoned with that we might very probably be visited by a spell of bad weather which would cut us off completely from the Peninsula for a fortnight or perhaps for even longer.

"Supplies, ammunition and material to a certain degree had therefore to be left to the last moment for fear of the isolation of the garrison at any moment when the evacuation might be in progress. I decided therefore that our aim should be primarily the withdrawal of the bulk of the personnel, artillery and ammunition in the intermediate period, and that no risks should be taken in prolonging the withdrawal of personnel at the final stage with a view to reducing the quantity of stores left.

"The entire evacuation of the Peninsula had now been completed. It demanded for its successful realization two important military essentials, viz., good luck and skilled disciplined organization, and they were both forthcoming to a marked degree at the hour needed. Our luck was in the ascendant by the marvellous spell of calm weather which prevailed. But we were able to turn to the fullest advantage these accidents of fortune."

The following is General Monro's review of the work done on the lines of communication in Gallipoli:—

"Before concluding this inadequate account of the events which happened during my tenure of command of the forces in the Eastern Mediterranean, I desire to give a brief explanation of the work which was carried out on the line of communications, and to replace on record my appreciation of the admirable work rendered by the officers responsible for this important service.

"On the Dardanelles Peninsula it may be said that the whole of the machinery by which the text-books contemplate the maintenance and supply of an army was non-existent. The zone commanded by the enemy's guns extended not only to the landing places on the Peninsula, but even over the sea in the vicinity.

"The beaches were the advanced depots and refilling points at which the services of supply had to be carried out under artillery fire. The landing of stores as well as of troops was only possible under cover of darkness.

"The sea, the ships, lighters and tugs took, in fact, the place of railways and roads, with their railway trains, mechanical transport, etc., but with this difference, that the use of the latter is subject only to the intervention of the enemy, while that of the former was dependent on the weather.

"Between the beaches and the base at Alexandria, 800 miles to the south, the line of communications had but two harbours, Kephalos Bay on the Island of Imbros, fifteen miles roughly from the beaches, and Mudros Bay, at a distance of sixty miles. In neither were there any piers, breakwaters, wharves, or store-houses of any description before the advent of the troops. On the shores of these two bays there were no roads of any military value, or buildings fit for military usage. The water supply at these islands was, until developed, totally inadequate for our needs.

"The Peninsula landing places were open beaches. Kephalos Bay is without protection from the north, and swept by a high sea in northerly gales. In Mudros Harbour, trans-shipments and disembarkations were often seriously impeded with a wind from the north or south. These difficulties were accentuated by the advent of submarines in the Ægean Sea, on account of which the Vice-Admiral deemed it necessary to prohibit any transport or store ship exceeding 1,500 tons proceeding north of Mudros, and although this rule was relaxed in the case of supply ships proceeding within the netted area of Suvla, it necessitated the trans-shipment of practically all reinforcements, stores and supplies—other than those for Suvla—into small ships in Mudros Harbour.

"At Suvla and Anzac disembarkation could only be effected by lighters and tugs, thus for all personnel and material there was at least one trans-shipment, and for the greater portion of both two trans-shipments.

"Yet notwithstanding the difficulties which have been set forth above, the Army was well maintained in equipment and ammunition. It was well fed, it received its full supply of winter clothing at the beginning of December. The evacuation of the sick and wounded was carried out with the minimum of inconvenience, and the provision of hospital accommodation for them on the Dardanelles line of communication and elsewhere in the Mediterranean met all requirements."

CHAPTER XVI.

COMMENTS TO FACILITATE THE STUDY OF THE CAMPAIGN ON THE OPERATIONS DESCRIBED IN CHAPTERS I TO XII.

Vide CHAPTER I: THE ENTRY OF TURKEY INTO THE WAR.

1. *Situation at the end of* 1914.—The Western Front had become stabilized. The most pressing problem now was how to relieve the pressure on the Russian army, as it was in difficulties both in Poland and in the Caucasus. It was thought that there would be no appreciable change for an indefinite period on the Western Front, so it was therefore hoped that the following objects would be derived from the Dardanelles campaign:—

(a) It would be possible to open up direct communication with Russia.

(b) Induce the Balkan States to join the Allies.

(c) Turn the left flank of the Central Powers.

2. *The Origin of this Campaign.*—There was a change in our war policy at the end of November. Now that there was static warfare on the Western Front the War Council considered the employment of the forces not actually required to hold the line on the Western Front. The Near East was, therefore, considered as a possible subsidiary area of operations. The War Council had full deliberative and executive powers. The real power, however, was in the hands of the Prime Minister, the Secretary of State for War, and the First Lord of the Admiralty.

3. *Proposals in December,* 1914.—Mr. Churchill proposed that there should be a combined naval and military attack on Constantinople via Gallipoli.

Another member of the War Council proposed to transfer the British Army to the Balkans.

Lord Kitchener inclined to the policy of being safe in the East and concentrating all available strength on the Western Front.

Lord Fisher suggested a naval and military attack on Schleswig-Holstein.

There was a lack of co-ordination of these views by the Prime Minister. There was little organization or preparation for a combined operation. There was no co-operation between the statesmen and naval and military experts in these views. There was no exhaustive combined report on any one of the suggested proposals by the Naval and Military Staffs. There was no General Staff at the Admiralty. A large proportion of the senior officers from the War Office had gone to France.

4. *Situation at the beginning of* 1915.—Italy was still hesitating as to its future policy. Serbia was isolated. Rumania and Greece were undecided. Bulgaria was coming under the influence of the Central Powers. Russia required assistance. Lord Kitchener promised to make a demonstration in the East to help Russia, but he considered that he would not be able to provide more than 150,000 men for land operations, and such a force could not, he estimated, be ready for several months, as he did not wish to weaken the forces in France or Egypt.

Mr. Churchill was optimistic as to the effect of purely naval operations in the Dardanelles.

On January 13th the Cabinet instructed the Admiralty to prepare for a naval expedition in February to bombard and seize Gallipoli, with Constantinople as the objective. It must be noted that these instructions were given for a purely naval operation at a time when the Cabinet was committed by Lord Kitchener's promise to assist Russia.

5. *Situation in February,* 1915.—When Greece refused to join the Allies, the Balkan project was rejected.

When the Turkish attack on the Suez Canal had failed by February 5th, Lord Kitchener was persuaded to allow the 29th Division to proceed to Gallipoli. The Royal Naval Division and a French division were also allotted for this campaign.

On February 16th the Cabinet decided that " the 29th Division was to be sent to Lemnos as early as possible. Colonial troops in Egypt were to be prepared for dispatch and the Admiralty was to collect necessary small craft at Alexandria." Thus a combined operation was now definitely started. However, the 29th Division was again withheld by Kitchener when the Russian situation became critical. This delay caused loss of time and secrecy in the concentration of the force.

Vide CHAPTER II: NAVAL OPERATIONS.

6. *Preliminary Naval Bombardments.*—(a) February 19th: Long-range fire was found to be inaccurate. The guns in the forts did not fire at long range. When the ships approached closer direct hits were registered on the outer forts of the Dardanelles. When the ships closed in to 3,000 yards the guns in the forts opened fire and apparently had not been hit.

(b) February 25th: The outer forts of the Dardanelles were

THE DARDANELLES CAMPAIGN 127

hit at long range. During the night the entrance to the channel was swept clear of mines.

(c) February 26th: The inner forts of the Dardanelles were engaged at 12,000 yards. There was no reply from the forts, but there was heavy fire from concealed howitzers and field guns. This fire forced our ships to keep on the move. Landing parties were able to destroy undamaged guns of the outer forts The numbers of mobile land guns of the Turks were found to have been considerably increased.

(d) March 18th: Naval attacks on the defences of the Narrows were carried out. The enemy released a large number of floating mines. Three of our ships were lost. It was now realized that the Navy could not force the Straits without military assistance. It was realized too that ships could not deal with concealed howitzers. This showed the value of dispersed mobile artillery on shore.

The ships' fire was handicapped by lack of aeroplane observation, and shortage of ammunition.

In order to obtain direct hits, anchoring was necessary. Mines and the fire of mobile howitzers prevented anchoring in the narrow waters. Thus it may be concluded that even poorly equipped coast defences can, in narrow waters, if supported by mines and mobile batteries, successfully deal with direct fire from modern warships; and that if shore batteries are to be destroyed by naval guns it will be necessary for ships to approach within short range and to be prepared to expend large quantities of ammunition.

After witnessing the bombardment of March 18th, Sir Ian Hamilton considered that the co-operation of his whole force would be necessary to enable the Fleet to achieve its first purpose.

7. *Cabinet Decision to Embark on Military Operations on a Large Scale.*—On March 22nd the Cabinet decided that the Straits must be forced and that large military operations must be undertaken if necessary.

8. *Summary.*—The British Empire was on March 22nd definitely committed to an amphibious operation in a subsidiary area of operations. The points militating against the possible success of this operation were as follows:—

(a) No detailed appreciations of the situation based on the combined deliberations of the experts of the fighting services or plans were drawn up before the Expeditionary Force arrived in the Ægean.

(b) The composition of the force and the preliminary instructions to the Commander-in-Chief showed that the views of G.H.Q., Western Front, that no subsidiary operation should be undertaken, would influence the conduct of operations and the dispatch of reinforcements. Sir Ian Hamilton, in speaking at Hull with reference to the lack of reinforcements, stated that " it was easier to get butter out of a dog's mouth than troops out of the War Office—except, that was to say, for the Western Front."

(c) Our communications and advanced base for operations at Gallipoli were not organized.
(d) There was a deficiency in the administrative services.
(e) There was delay in the arrival of the 29th Division.
(f) No administrative staff work was done before leaving England.
(g) Transports were improperly loaded.
(h) The reloading of the transports at Alexandria caused delay, so that there was loss of secrecy, a consequent strengthening of the enemy's defences, and surprise was no longer possible.
(i) There was lack of co-ordination and unity of purpose at the inception of the campaign.
(j) The effect of naval guns against coast defences was over-estimated.

Vide CHAPTER III: PLAN OF CAMPAIGN.

9. In the orders issued on April 13th for the operations necessary to carry out the Commander-in-Chief's plan, the probable degree of resistance by the Turks was not indicated. It may be assumed that the General Staff considered that naval gunfire would enable the troops to land without resistance.

10. The orders for naval co-operation were worked out in great detail. Clear arrangements were made for beach organization and for inter-communication.

A separate squadron was provided for each main landing and feint, namely: the 29th Division was to be landed on five beaches at the southern end of the Peninsula for the main attack to be directed on Achi Baba from Cape Helles; for the Anzac Corps to land near Gaba Tepe; for subsidiary feints to be made by (a) a French brigade at Kum Kale to draw off artillery fire from the main operation at Helles and to stop Turkish reinforcements from coming to the Peninsula from the Asiatic coast, and (b) the R.N. Division at Bulair to alarm the Turkish Government at Constantinople and to mislead their commander in the field.

11. The orders for the covering force (seven battalions, one

THE DARDANELLES CAMPAIGN

field company and one field ambulance) gave Achi Baba as the objective; there was, however, no indication as to the immediate action of this force on landing, nor was there a fire plan beyond the statement that the covering ships would bombard the southern end of the Peninsula at daybreak.

Vide CHAPTER IV: THE LANDINGS.

12. The feint at Bulair was successful. Two Turkish divisions were retained near Gallipoli, and thus were diverted from our main operations.

The Bulair lines were bombarded, Bakla Bay was swept for mines, and 1,200 men were towed off shore at dusk.

13. The feint at Kum Kale was successful. Two Turkish divisions with their guns were retained on the Asiatic coast and were thus diverted from the main landings.

The Kum Kale forts were bombarded and, though the landing was delayed by opposition, it was effectively carried out by 1000 hours.

14. The landing at " S " Beach (Morto Bay) was very well carried out and had useful results. Although touch was not obtained with the troops attempting to land at " V " Beach, yet the right flank of the main operation was protected, and Turkish reinforcements were prevented from coming down to Sedd-el-Bahr where the landing at " V " Beach had been unsuccessful. Throughout this landing naval co-operation was most effective.

The 2nd Bn. The South Wales Borderers (less one company) and a detachment of the 2nd London Field Company, R.E., landed at Eski Hissarlik. The sea approach was difficult, the beach was narrow and had been entrenched by the Turkish company in the vicinity. The troops were embarked in four trawlers, each towing six cutters.

The position was stormed and captured by 0830 hours. This isolated position was held for two days, when it was occupied by the French troops.

15. " *V* " *Beach.*—The attempt to land the 2,100 men in the collier *River Clyde* at this beach proved to be a costly experiment. The exit doors of this ship became a defile at close range to the enemy. It would in all probability have been more advisable to have tried this experiment under cover of darkness. The Turks held their fire until the *River Clyde* was beached at close range. The troops were shot down as they left the ship. Few men survived and crossed the beach to shelter in dead ground. The remainder of the troops for " V " Beach were diverted to " W " Beach, and efforts to clear the *River Clyde* were suspended until dusk.

K*

16. "*W*" *Beach*.—This beach was most favourable for defence and therefore it was not advisable to use it for a landing in broad daylight.

The success of the troops landing on the rocks at Cape Tekke shows the advantage of getting ashore at unlikely and unattractive landing-places.

The state of the enemy's wire and trenches after the bombardment afforded proof of the difficulties and ineffectiveness of ships' gunfire against such land targets.

At 0600 hours the 1st Bn. The Lancashire Fusiliers were landed in eight tows in line abreast. H.M.Ss. *Swiftsure* and *Albion* gave covering fire. The Turks opened destructive fire as soon as the steamboats slipped tows. There were many casualties in the boats and while landing over wire. A company on the left flank managed to get a footing under the cliff and turned the flank of the Turks on the beach.

The Worcestershire Regiment, arrived at 0930 hours, and by midday gained touch with the Royal Fusiliers on "X" Beach.

17. "*X*" *Beach*.—The successful landing at this beach was largely due to the close support of the naval guns and to the enemy being unprepared for a landing at this beach and to their siting of the trenches on the edge of the cliff. H.M.S. *Implacable* reached a position 450 yards from the beach and maintained intensive fire on the Turkish line of trenches.

The Royal Fusiliers in H.M.S. *Implacable* and two Fleet sweepers stood in at 0400 hours. Companies were landed without a casualty in four tows of six boats each.

The Royal Fusiliers tried to join up with flank formations, but were unable to capture Hill 114 until 1230 hours.

18. "*Y*" *Beach*.—Although a landing at this beach appeared relatively uninviting owing to the steepness and height of the cliffs, yet actually it was easily accomplished. A larger force might have been successfully landed at this beach, as the Turks evidently considered that the difficulty of the country precluded a landing in force. Re-embarkation was successfully carried out under cover of the ships' guns.

The troops landing at this beach contained one and a half Turkish battalions during the vital struggle at Helles.

The advanced party of two companies of the 1st Bn. The King's Own Scottish Borderers in four trawlers, supported by naval fire, landed unopposed.

The whole force of two battalions and a company was ashore by 0715 hours. Part of this force crossed Gully Ravine. There were persistent counter-attacks by troops of the Turks' 9th Division.

On the following morning—April 26th—our force was re-embarked.

THE DARDANELLES CAMPAIGN

19. *The A. and N.Z. Corps Landing.*—This landing took place under cover of darkness. The tows missed the intended landing-place by a mile. This was due to the strong current running at the time. This turned out to be fortunate at first, as, although the cliffs were steep in the area, in which the covering force landed, yet there were only a few Turks in the trenches on the beach and on the side of the cliffs.

Failure to make more ground at first was due to the difficulty of the country and to the units being separated after landing.

The covering force approached the coast at 0300 hours. There were 1,500 men in battleships and 2,500 men in eight destroyers. Tows were cast off at 0330 hours and carried by current northwards. They were beached at 0425 hours close to cliffs 300 feet high. The whole covering force was ashore by 0530 hours. The cliffs overlooking the landing-place were secured at the first assault. Eight thousand troops were ashore by 0730 hours.

Three brigades and two batteries of mountain artillery were ashore by 1400 hours. By 1800 hours 15,000 had been landed. By 1500 hours Essad Pasha had concentrated the 19th Division from Boghali in the vicinity of the Anzac position. Heavy counter-attacks were repulsed with difficulty.

The Commander-in-Chief decided that the position must be retained.

20. *Situation after dark on April 25th.*—A. and N.Z. Corps were fighting stubbornly. Their situation was not secure or satisfactory.

At Helles the 29th Division was on a two-mile front from " W " Beach to " X " Beach. There had been heavy losses and no progress at " V " Beach.

The Turks were being reinforced.

21. *General Comments.*—(*a*) Failure to gain ground at the outset paralysed subsequent action.

(*b*) The three beaches selected for the main landing at Helles together afforded only 900 yards frontage. This was very narrow in view of the necessity of getting large numbers ashore as early as possible and of obtaining depth to the positions.

(*c*) Naval gunfire was not so effective in support of the troops landing at the principal beaches—namely, " V " and " W "—as at the remainder of the landing-places.

(*d*) If some portable guns had been available and had been landed with the troops at Anzac, they would have been invaluable.

(*e*) The value of surprise was well illustrated by the landings at Helles and Anzac. At Anzac, although the troops were landed at the wrong place, they had a considerable initial advantage, although later they encountered abnormal topographical difficulties.

(f) Owing to command of the sea the initiative and liberty of action were possible for our force.

The principles of war inculcate the necessity of striking with all available strength at one decisive point. It must then be considered if this would have been possible or not, and if it had been possible could not the enemy, seeing where we had concentrated, have brought all their forces to bear at this point?

The answer to the question depends on time and space, on boat accommodation, and on beach space.

Examination of the available factors after the event leads to the conclusion that the entire force could have been landed north of Gaba Tepe in one day with the shipping at our disposal.

This place would have been better than the limited and overlooked beaches at Helles, and it would have been within striking distance of the objective—the Narrows.

The Turks could not have concentrated their entire strength on one day to meet our attack. Therefore, we should have had numerical superiority and we should have thus carried out the principle of concentrating superior numbers at the decisive time and place if our force had been landed north of Gaba Tepe on April 25th.

22. *The Points for Consideration at the War Council's Meeting on May 14th, 1915, were*:—

    (a) That the landings had been carried out, but that the main objectives had not been reached.

    (b) Our casualties, exclusive of those incurred by the French, were 14,000.

    (c) That drafts and reinforcements must be sent out to another area where there would only be trench warfare.

    (d) That the expenditure of ammunition, especially in H.E., would be considerable, and that it had not been foreseen.

    (e) That the demands of the Western Front and of other areas of operations were increasing.

    (f) That the Dardanelles operations, if continued, must be subsidiary.

    (g) That if the operations were not continued there would be a loss of prestige throughout the East.

    (h) That it was important to continue our operations if neutral Powers were to be influenced.

THE DARDANELLES CAMPAIGN 133

Vide CHAPTER *VII*: OPERATIONS UP TO THE END OF JUNE.
Dardanelles Committee.

23. The opinion expressed in the appreciation of the situation by Lord Kitchener was for the continuance of operations.

24. The Dardanelles Committee decided on June 7th to send to Gallipoli three New Army divisions and some additional naval units. A subsequent decision was to send also two Territorial divisions. These reinforcements were to arrive between July 10th and August 10th. The French were also sending a second division to General Gourand.

25. The delay in the dispatch of these reinforcements seriously prejudiced the chances of success.

Employment of Reinforcements in a New Offensive.

26. *Concentration in the Helles Area.*—It was considered that the Turkish defences were too strong, the positions were too confined, and the enemy's reserves were too close.

27. *Disembarkation on the Asiatic Coast followed by a March on Chanak.*—This was rejected, as a simultaneous offensive on the Peninsula would have been necessary, and there were not enough troops for both operations.

28. *Landing near Bulair.*—The beaches were not suitable for landing operations in this area. There would be additional distance for the sea journey, which was not so safe as formerly owing to German submarines.

29. *Landing at Suvla Bay and to reinforce Anzac,* with the first objective to be Sari Bair, and thence the positions dominating the Narrows. This operation gave the best prospects of success. A landing in this area would be nearer the Narrows than at any of the other alternative places considered as possible. The ground facilitated concealment. Suvla Bay was sheltered.

30. *Decision.*—It was decided to create a new base in Suvla Bay and to advance from Anzac with Sari Bair as a first objective. Reinforcements were to be collected in and north of the Anzac position. The final objective was to be a position astride the Peninsula from the vicinity of Gaba Tepe to the north of Maidos.

Vide CHAPTER IX: OFFENSIVE OPERATIONS AT ANZAC AND HELLES.

31. *Details of the Plan for the August Offensive, to commence on August 6th.*—(*a*) The main attack was to be made from Anzac. The first objectives were the summits of Sari

Bair. Thence the attack was to be carried forward east and south-east to Maidos and the Kilid Bahr Plateau. The Turks would be prepared to meet direct attacks. Therefore, it was wisely decided to carry out night operations, and to gain the advantage of a surprise attack. The plan, then, was to march the attacking force north from Anzac, wheel to the east and assault Sari Bair from the north-west. Subsidiary attacks were to be made from the right and centre of the Anzac position in order to contain the enemy in this area and to gain ground.

(*b*) The 29th, 42nd, 52nd, R.N. and French Divisions were also to make an attack at Helles in order to contain the Turks in that area and divert their attention from the main operations at Anzac and Suvla Bay. Also it was hoped to gain ground and to improve the positions.

(*c*) The landing at Suvla Bay of the 10th Division (less the 29th Brigade) and of the 11th Division was to be a surprise. The bulk of the infantry were to be landed under cover of darkness. The object of these operations was to secure a new base and to co-operate on the left of the offensive operations being carried out at Anzac.

32. *Preparations for the August Offensive.*—(*a*) The enemy were to be misled as to our intentions by demonstrations south of Gaba Tepe and along the Asiatic coast, by concentrations at Mitylene, and by a temporary landing in the Gulf of Saros.

(*b*) During the nights of August 4th, 5th and 6th, 10,000 additional troops were concentrated at Anzac.

Arrangements were made with the Navy for the co-ordinated movements of the 10th and 11th Divisions from Mudros, Imbros and Mitylene.

33. *Turkish Dispositions.*—Within the area of operations the Turkish 3rd, 4th, 5th, 7th, 8th, 9th, 11th, 12th, 15th and 19th Divisions were identified. Their local reserves were in the vicinity of Maidos. Their reserve group was near Bulair. In the Suvla area there were only three battalions.

34. *The Helles Operations.*—These operations fulfilled their objective by containing the Turks in the Helles area, but there was little gain of ground owing to lack of artillery preparation. It was found, also, that searching howitzer fire was required to deal with the Turks' overhead cover and deep trenches.

On the afternoon of August 6th the main attack was delivered near the centre of the Turkish front. Subsidiary attacks on our left flank gained ground. Our main effort was repulsed, but the enemy's offensive on the whole front was forestalled.

The Turkish counter-attack on August 7th was repulsed. By

THE DARDANELLES CAMPAIGN

August 13th the vineyard west of the road leading to Krithia had been several times lost before being finally recaptured. The French divisions had severe fighting on the right flank.

35. The Anzac Operations.

(a) *Preparations.*—The Turks were quite unprepared for large-scale operations in this area. The concentration of troops, their mule transport, their extra stores of ammunition, food, their water tanks and pumps was successfully concealed from the enemy for three days.

(b) *Subsidiary Operations.*—On the afternoon of August 6th an attack was carried out against the Turkish trenches on Lone Pine by the 1st Australian Brigade. There was severe fighting and heavy losses were incurred. Although no considerable progress was made owing to lack of artillery preparation and trench mortars, yet large numbers of Turks who might have been available on other parts of the front were contained.

(c) *Main Operations.*—The country in which the fighting took place was extremely intricate for night operations. The attacking troops were divided into two groups for the approach march. Each group was sub-divided into covering and assaulting columns.

Operations started on the evening of August 6th. The right covering column, after capturing Table Top, was to open up Chailak and Sazli Beit Ravines for the assaulting column, which was then to capture Chunuk Bair. The left covering column, after seizing Damakjelik Bair, was to open up Aghyl Dere for the assaulting column, which was then to capture Hill 305. There was a reserve of six battalions.

The right covering column captured No. 3 Post by strategem at 2130 hours, and Table Top by 0100 hours. The right assaulting column reached the upper slopes of Sari Bair Ridge. The left assaulting column reached the lower slopes of Hill Q after dealing with strong opposition.

At 0700 hours on August 7th New Zealand and Australian troops held Rhododendron Spur. The 29th Indian Infantry Brigade were in Aghyl Dere.

On August 8th there was much fighting with heavy losses on both sides.

On August 9th the attacks on Chunuk Bair were renewed after preliminary naval bombardment. There was good progress at first and the ridge was captured, but it was not held on the following day, when, by strong counter-attacks, the Turks recovered Chunuk Bair. The 13th Division had now lost over sixty per cent. and the A. and N.Z. Corps had lost thirty-five per cent. casualties.

The causes of the failure to gain the objective appear to have been that the initial progress was too slow, and the numbers finally available were insufficient. The weather and water supply added to the difficulties of the operation.

Vide CHAPTER X: OPERATIONS AT SUVLA BAY.

36. *Suvla Operations.*

(a) *August 6th and 7th.*—The initial landing was to be made by the 11th Division followed by half the 10th Division. The objectives were first to secure Suvla Bay as a base and then to occupy the eastern slopes of 305 Hill.

The flotilla sailed from Imbros at 1900 hours on August 6th. The 32nd and 33rd Brigades landed at 2000 hours without opposition at " B " and " C " Beaches. The 34th Brigade, landing inside Suvla Bay at " A " Beach, was opposed and had to wade ashore.

Two mountain batteries and four 15-pounders were landed at " B " Beach by 0530 hours on August 7th. Part of the 30th Brigade and the 31st Brigade landed at " C " Beach at dawn. The remainder of the 30th Brigade landed near Ghazi Baba and moved up the coast.

The advance of the 11th Division towards Ismail Oglu Tepe was slow, as there were considerable difficulties as to water supply, and the troops were exhausted, and units were somewhat mixed up. Their attack opened at 1715 hours. Chocolate Hill was captured at 1830 hours. No further progress was made.

(b) *Final Offensive Operations at Suvla.*—On August 8th little progress was made. Two divisions of the Turks were on the way from Bulair. The Turks temporarily withdrew their guns from Anafarta Ridge.

The Commander-in-Chief visited the Suvla area at 1700 hours. Orders were then issued for an advance against the enemy's positions at Anafarta.

The 32nd Brigade attacked at 0400 hours on August 9th. Turkish reinforcements had begun to arrive by this time. Our attack was repulsed.

The 53rd Division arrived on August 9th, and the 54th Division landed on August 11th.

No further progress was made on August 15th along the Kiretch Tepe Sirt. The offensive operations against the Turkish positions on Ismail Oglu Tepe on August 21st were not successful.

37. *General Comments on the August Offensive.*—The conception was sound, as the occupation of the Kilid Bahr

Plateau was the key to the Straits. No better scheme could have been devised. It would not have been possible to gain the objective from Helles or from the right of the Anzac position. The causes of failure must, however, be considered. They were: —

- (a) The estimate of the capabilities of the troops carrying out the offensive was too optimistic.
- (b) Owing to the intricacies of the country and the opposition encountered, the summits of Sari Bair were too difficult an objective to be attained by daybreak on August 7th.
- (c) That the 11th Division, after landing, could capture positions on the Anafarta Heights on August 7th was a too sanguine forecast, as there were so many difficulties with reference to water supply.
- (d) The first cause of failure was that the Anzac force could not capture the Sari Bair Heights on August 7th, owing to the difficulty of the country and the left column missing its direction.
- (e) The second cause must have been that the IX Corps did not advance on August 8th, as later Turkish reinforcements then occupied positions covering their advance.

38. *General Comments on the Campaign up to the Final Offensive Operations.*—(a) The area of operations selected for our offensive operations towards Constantinople favoured the defence, as all the forward movements by our troops were over uphill, broken ground covered with dense scrub giving good·cover to the defenders. There was no observation for the attackers to cover their advance by fire; consolidation was difficult owing to the heavy soil; there was lack of land artillery support and aeroplane observation.

(b) The Commander-in-Chief had to form his plans in accordance with the arrival of reinforcements.

(c) The failure of the Anzac force to capture the Sari Bair Heights on August 7th was the first cause of the failure of the plan.

(d) The other main reason was the failure of the IX Corps to advance on August 8th, as Turkish reinforcements then began to arrive in the area of operations.

39. *Situation after the August Offensive.*—(a) After the August offensive reinforcements were asked for and refused. The enemy had superior numbers and possessed all the tactical advantages. Winter was approaching with the storms

threatening our communications. Our troops were tired and depleted. Morale would suffer owing to lack of rest, disease, climatic conditions varying from periods of extreme heat and dust to those of blizzard and floods, shortage of water, monotony of food, lack of reinforcements, ammunition and ordnance stores.

(b) In short, the campaign was being carried out under most unfavourable general conditions. The redeeming feature was the tenacity of all ranks.

(c) The Allied offensive on the Western Front had failed; the Serbian Army had retreated; Bulgaria had mobilized.

An expedition to Salonika was being arranged. Two divisions were to be taken from Gallipoli for this expedition.

(d) General Sir C. Monro was appointed to report fully on whether the Peninsula should be evacuated or whether further offensive operations should be undertaken.

(e) General Monro recommended evacuation.

(f) It was finally decided, after Lord Kitchener's inspection of the positions of the Peninsula, and after the storms followed by blizzards starting on November 21st, to carry out this recommendation.

Vide CHAPTER XI: OPERATIONS AND PLANS LEADING TO THE EVACUATION.

40. *Evacuation.*—The problem was how to withdraw thirteen divisions, namely, 83,000 men, 5,000 animals, 200 guns and 2,000 vehicles from close proximity to the enemy, and then to re-embark them on open beaches within range of the Turks' guns. The Turks had received additional artillery and ammunition.

It was probable that Turkish airmen would discover the first signs of evacuation during the preliminary stages. In the event of the discovery of our plans, artillery fire on to our beaches would have been most serious.

Success was based on weather conditions being favourable, on efficient organization carried out with precision, on preventing the Turkish commanders from even suspecting our intentions, and on deception of the enemy in the forward trenches up till the last moment.

The general scheme of the evacuation was:

- (a) That measures were to be taken to preserve a normal appearance in the areas of Suvla and Anzac during daylight.
- (b) That all troops, animals and stores not required for a long campaign were to be withdrawn during the hours of darkness between December 10th and 17th.

THE DARDANELLES CAMPAIGN

(c) That all personnel and material not required for defence in case of unavoidable delay in carrying out the plan was to be withdrawn on the night of December 18th/19th.

(d) That the final evacuation on the night of December 19th/20th of the remainder of the personnel and material would be secretly and rapidly carried out.

Vide CHAPTER XII: THE EVACUATION.

41. *Evacuation at Anzac and Suvla.*—(a) At Suvla a system of emergency defensive lines were constructed with strong posts at the beach extremities.

(b) During the night of December 19th/20th re-embarkation took place in four stages; motor-lighters were used for the re-embarkation.

At 1930 hours the last gun was removed. By 2145 hours only 800 rifles remained in the forward positions holding 4,500 yards of trenches.

At 2345 hours all trench mortars were removed.

At 0115 hours the front line of trenches had been vacated. Two hundred rifles occupied the fourth line as a rearguard.

At 0515 hours this rearguard embarked at Suvla Cove.

Stores were fired. The casualties were two men wounded.

At 0700 hours the Turkish guns opened fire on the beaches at Suvla.

(c) At Anzac the final withdrawal was made in three groups, leaving 2,000 men in the forward positions.

At 0300 hours numbers in forward positions were reduced to 800.

By 0330 hours Lone Pine, Pope's and Quinn's Posts were vacated, and a final rush down the ravines to the beach was made.

At 0345 hours a mine containing three and a half tons of ammonal was exploded at the Neck. The Turks, then evidently expecting an attack, shelled the empty front-line trenches.

The casualties were three men wounded. Preparations had been made at Mudros for 10,000 wounded.

42. *Evacuation of Helles.*—(a) Again owing to the excellent naval arrangements, combined with efficient staff work and precise plans carried out by the troops without a hitch, the evacuation was successfully carried out. The motor-lighters, as at Suvla, were a great success for the re-embarkation of the troops. The weather conditions just remained favourable until the last troops were on board.

(b) The problem at Helles was to re-embark 40,000 men, 4,500 animals, 150 guns and 1,000 tons of stores.

(c) The French troops were embarked between January 1st and 4th, having been relieved by Royal Naval Division.

The 42nd Division was withdrawn from the front line for rest. The 13th and 29th Divisions were transferred to Helles.

(d) The afternoon of January 8th was fine with a light breeze. Four battalions of each of the 13th, 29th, 52nd and Royal Naval Divisions were left to be embarked in three groups.

No. 1 Group embarked at 1900 hours in destroyers and beetles. The wind was beginning to rise.

No. 2 Group embarked by midnight.

The rearguard reached the beaches by 0230 hours.

The beaches were cleared by 0330 hours under great difficulties owing to the rising wind and strong sea now running. Seventeen thousand men and 35 guns had been withdrawn during this night; 17 guns and 508 animals had to be abandoned.

43. *Main Causes of Failure.*—(a) Naval attacks precluded the possibility of surprise and gave the enemy warning of our intended attack.

(b) Delay in concentration of military forces for land attack due to:—

    (i) Original plan to force the Straits by the Navy alone.

    (ii) Retention of the 29th Division.

    (iii) Necessity for reloading transports.

(c) Under-estimation of the Turks' fighting capacity and morale.

(d) The military expedition not being properly equipped as regards:—

    (i) First reinforcements.

    (ii) Howitzers, trench mortars, and ammunition.

    (iii) Administrative services.

(e) Difficulties of country in which the operations were to take place.

44. *Main Lessons of the Campaign.*—(a) The necessity of making beforehand an exhaustive appreciation of the situation from a naval and military point of view leading to a definite plan of operations.

THE DARDANELLES CAMPAIGN

(*b*) The influence of submarines on amphibious warfare with modern armies containing greater numbers and requiring much greater fire support than formerly.

(*c*) The comparative ineffectiveness of ordinary naval gunfire against shore targets.

(*d*) The necessity of having reserves available on the spot in distant campaigns.

INDEX

A

Abrikja, xii, 61, 63.
Achi Baba, viii, 2, 4, 16, 18, 23, 24, 30, 32, 33, 35, 37, 38, 41, 45, 49, 101.
Adriatic, 40.
Adrianople, 9, 89.
Admiralty, 6, 9, 32, 92, 126.
Ægean Sea, 92, 123, 127.
Agamemnon, H.M.S., 7.
Aghyl Dere, 53, 54, 55, 56, 135.
Aire Kavak, 68.
Albion, H.M.S., 25, 95.
Aleppo, 1.
Alexandretta, 89.
Alexandria, vi, 15, 17, 92, 93, 128.
Alps, The, 2, 5.
Allies, The, x, 1, 9, 47, 52, 69, 89, 99, 125, 133, 138.
Anafarta Sagir, xii, 54, 57, 60, 62, 63, 64, 67, 69, 109, 136, 137.
Anzac, ix, x, xv, xvi, 2, 20, 29, 31, 32, 33, 45, 47, 51, 52, 59, 61, 67, 69, 70, 74, 75, 109, 131.
Anzac Corps, vi, viii, x, xiv, 16, 17, 19, 20, 21, 32, 38, 44, 47, 48, 49, 53, 56, 57, 58, 68, 69, 90, 92, 98, 99, 131, 135.
Archangel, 1.
Ari Burnu, 20, 94.
Asia Minor, 1, 9, 12, 16, 90.
Asiatic Coast, 27, 47.
Athens, 89, 90.
Aubers Ridge, 37.
Auckland Mounted Rifles, 55, 56.
Austria, 6, 9.
Azmak Dere, xi, xiii, xiv, 55, 56, 64, 66, 68, 69.

B

Baby Post, 22, 53, 99, 109.
B.11 (submarine), v, 8, 89.
Bakla Bay, 93, 129.
Balkan States, v, 2, 4.
Bauchop's Hill, 55.
Beach "A," xi, 59, 60, 109, 136.
Beach "B," xi, 59, 109.
Beach "C," xi, 59, 60, 109, 136.
Berlin, 8.
Besika Bay, 15, 93.
Birdwood, General Sir William, 32, 50, 95, 116.

Black Sea, 8, 47.
Boghali, 15, 131.
Bolton's Ridge, 29, 94.
Boomerang Trench, 106.
Border Regiment, 27, 44, 45, 96, 106, 107.
Bosphorus, The, 12, 91, 103.
Breslau (Turkish ship), v, 8.
Brigades, 1st Metropolitan (French), 80.
Brigade, 1st Naval, 84.
Brigade, 1st South Midland, 87.
Brigade, 1st Australian, 15, 21, 80, 135.
Brigade, 2nd Australian, x, 15, 20, 21, 35, 55, 80, 94.
Brigade, 1st Australian Light Horse, 15, 53, 81.
Brigade, 2nd Australian Light Horse, 82.
Brigade, 2nd Colonial (French), 80.
Brigade, 2nd South Midland, 87.
Brigade, 3rd Australian, 15, 35, 36, 37, 81.
Brigade, 3rd Australian Light Horse, 82.
Brigade, 3rd Metropolitan (French), 80.
Brigade, 3rd Notts and Derby, 87.
Brigade, 4th Australian, xi, 15, 54, 55, 56, 81, 97.
Brigade, 4th Colonial (French), 80.
Brigade, 5th Australian, 81.
Brigade, 6th Australian, 81.
Brigade, 7th Australian, 82.
Brigade, 29th Brigade, 50, 51, 53, 59, 84.
Brigade, 29th Indian, xiv, 15, 34, 39, 43, 44, 45, 47, 54, 55, 56, 69, 75, 99, 135.
Brigade, 30th, xii, 60, 65, 84.
Brigade, 31st, xii, 63, 65, 84.
Brigade, 32nd, xi, xii, 60, 61, 63, 68, 85, 136.
Brigade, 33rd, xi, xii, 68, 85.
Brigade, 34th, xi, xii, 59, 60, 63, 68, 85.
Brigade, 39th, 56, 85.
Brigade, 86th, 15, 45, 82.
Brigade, 87th, 15, 30, 34, 36, 82.
Brigade, 88th, 15, 30, 35, 36, 83.
Brigade, 125th, 15, 35, 36, 37, 45, 83.
Brigade, 126th, 15, 83.

INDEX

Brigade, 127th, 15, 39, 42, 43, 83, 104.
Brigade, 155th, 48, 83.
Brigade, 157th, 48, 84.
Brigade, 162nd, xiii, 86.
Brighton Beach, 44.
Britain, v, 1, 5, 37, 89.
Bulair, ix, 2, 7, 12, 15, 17, 20, 47, 50, 91, 93, 128, 129, 136.
Bulgaria, 3, 90, 126, 138.
Bulgarians, 6, 9.

C

Camber Beach, vi, 25, 26, 95.
Carden, Admiral, 90, 91.
Carpathians, 40.
Cattaro, 40.
Caucasus Mountains, 5, 9.
Chailak, 53, 54, 55, 57, 58, 109.
Chanak, 7, 10, 12, 13, 14, 49, 52, 133.
Chatalja Lines, 47.
Chatham Post, 75.
Chocolate Hill, xi, xii, 30, 60, 61, 62, 63, 67, 68, 69, 70, 74, 89, 92, 95, 96, 114, 127, 136, 137.
Chunuk Bair, viii, xi, 20, 21, 38, 54, 55, 56, 57, 58, 69, 70, 94, 115, 116, 135.
Churchill, W., The Right Hon., 3, 126.
Colne, H.M.S., 55, 99.
Commander-in-Chief, x, xi, xii, xiii, 16, 17, 19, 52, 54, 56, 93.
Constantinople, v, viii, 6, 9, 16, 31, 40, 45, 47, 72, 126, 128, 137.
Cornwallis, H.M.S., 25, 95.
Corps, VIII, 52, 78, 103.
Corps, IX, ix, xi, 54, 59, 61, 62, 64, 65, 66, 137.
Courtney's Post, 98.
Cox, H. V., General, 56, 69, 117.

D

Dalmatia, 9.
d'Amade, General, 27, 36.
Damakjelik Bair, xi, xiv, 54, 55, 58, 68, 69.
Dardanelles, v, viii, 1, 3, 4, 5, 6, 7, 8, 9, 10, 31, 47, 49, 70, 71, 90, 91, 92, 106, 123, 126, 127, 131, 132, 133.
Dardanus, vi, 11, 12, 13.
de Lisle, General, 65, 67.
de Robeck, Admiral, 15.
Division, 1st French, ix, 15, 42, 47, 80.
Division, 2nd French, ix, 36, 42, 43, 80.
Division, 1st Australian, 80, 81.
Division, 2nd Australian, xiv, 47, 69, 81.
Division, 2nd Mounted, 47, 67, 68, 69, 87.
Division, A.N.Z., 15, 53, 81.
Division, 10th, x, xiii, 47, 50, 51, 60, 61, 64, 65, 66, 68, 69, 71.
Division, 11th, xi, xii, xiv, 47, 50, 59, 60, 61, 64, 65, 66, 68, 110, 112, 136, 137.
Division, 13th, xiv, xv, 47, 51, 53, 55, 59, 69, 121, 135, 140.
Division, 29th, ix, xiii, xiv, 10, 12, 15, 16, 19, 30, 31, 34, 35, 38, 39, 42, 44, 47, 67, 68, 69, 90, 91, 92, 101, 126, 128, 134, 140.
Division, 42nd, vii, 35, 39, 42, 47, 99, 105, 134, 140.
Division, 52nd, viii, 41, 47, 103, 107, 134.
Division, 53rd, xii, xiii, 47, 64, 66, 68, 114, 115, 136.
Division, 54th, xiii, 47, 65, 66, 68.

E

E.14 (British submarine), 97.
E.15 (British submarine), 14, 93.
Egypt, xiii, 1, 5, 15, 35, 90, 91, 92.
England, 39, 48, 67.
Enos, 14, 17, 50.
Enver, Pasha, 45.
Eren Keui, 7.
Essad, Pasha, 15, 98, 131.
Eski Hissarlik, vii, 7, 23, 30.
Euryalus, H.M.S., 26, 96.

F

Fao, 1.
Festubert, 37.
Fir Tree Spur, 101, 104.
Fir Tree Wood, 35, 36, 105.
Fisher, Admiral of the Fleet, v, 3, 9, 89, 125.
Fisherman's Hut, 20, 53, 94.
Fort Orkanie, 10.
Fort Soghandere, 11, 12, 13.
Foxhound, H.M.S., 65.
France, 9, 38, 39.
French Corps, ix, 15, 38, 43, 46, 47, 48, 135.
French Government, 70, 89, 133.
French Troops, 27, 36, 39, 51, 92, 100.

INDEX

G

Gaba Tepe, vi, ix, xiv, 7, 14, 18, 19, 20, 21, 31, 33, 41, 51, 69, 94, 133.
Galicia, viii, 5, 40.
Gallipoli, v, viii, xiv, xv, 1, 4, 5, 6, 7, 8, 15, 17, 31, 37, 38, 40, 46, 47, 48, 52, 62, 67, 70, 71, 72, 89, 92, 128, 133.
Germany, 1, 2, 4, 6.
Ghazi Baba, 60.
Godley, General Sir A., 45, 108.
Gœben (Turkish battleship), v, 8, 89.
Goliath, H.M.S., 24, 40.
Grampus, H.M.S., 65.
Greece, 1, 6, 90.
Green Hill, xii, xiii, 60, 61, 64, 69.
Guépratte, Admiral, 15.
Gully Beach, xvi, 76.
Gully Ravine, 30, 93, 107, 130.
Gully Spur, 78, 107.
Gurkhas, 1/5th, 39, 108.
Gurkhas, 1/6th, 108.
Gurkhas, 2/10th, 108.

H

Haifa, 89.
Hamilton, General Sir Ian, vi, viii, xiv, 12, 15, 17, 22, 31, 32, 35, 36, 37, 38, 39, 40, 41, 50, 60, 61, 62, 63, 64, 71, 91, 92, 103, 127.
Haricot Redoubt, ix, 44, 104.
Helles, vi, vii, viii, ix, xiii, xvi, 2, 4, 7, 10, 16, 18, 19, 22, 23, 26, 27, 28, 30, 31, 32, 33, 34, 35, 38, 39, 44, 45, 46, 47, 51, 52, 67, 73, 76, 77, 97, 121, 131, 133, 134, 137, 138, 139, 140.
Hetman Chair, xiii, 68.
Hill 10, xi, 59, 60.
Hill 60, 69, 75.
Hill 70, xii, 63, 114.
Hill 114, 18, 26, 27, 96, 97, 130.
Hill 138, 18, 26, 27, 97.
Hill 141, vii, 18.
Hill 236, 30, 98.
Hill 305, xi, 55, 56.
Hill 472, 30, 98.
Hill 700, 53.
Hill 971, 20.
Hill Q, 35, 55, 57, 135.

I

Imbros, 59, 76, 124.
Implacable, H.M.S., 27.
Inflexible, H.M.S., 7, 13.
Inniskilling Fusiliers, 27, 96, 108.
Ismail Oglu Tepe, xi, xii, 60, 63, 67, 109, 136.
Italy, 6, 126.

J

Joffre, Marshal, 90.
Jonquil, H.M.S., 112.

K

Kabal Kuyu, xiv, 68, 69, 117.
Karakol Dagh, xi, 59, 60, 61, 109, 110.
Kavak Tepe, xiii, 64, 110.
Kephalos Bay, 124.
Kephez Point, 11, 13, 14.
Kereves Dere, ix, 34, 35, 36, 42, 43, 44, 46, 47, 48, 98, 101.
Kilid Bahr, 7, 12, 13, 16, 49, 98, 105, 134, 136.
Kiretch Tepe Sirt, xii, xiii, xiv, 61, 64, 66, 68, 69, 115, 136.
Kirte Dere, 30, 99, 105, 108.
Kitchener, Earl, viii, 3, 9, 10, 12, 16, 39, 42, 74, 90, 91, 92, 103, 125, 126, 138.
King's Own Scottish Borderers, 1st Bn., 23, 130.
King's Own Scottish Borderers, 4th Bn., 48, 98, 115.
Knoll, The, 45, 46.
Krithia, vii, 4, 29, 30, 31, 32, 33, 34, 35, 37, 44, 45, 46, 48, 71, 98, 100, 104.
Kuchuk Anafarta Ova, xi, xii, xiii, 63, 64, 66.
Kum Kale, vi, 7, 10, 11, 12, 17, 18, 19, 27, 28, 29, 44, 91, 93, 94, 96, 128, 129.
Kum Tepe, 51.

L

Lala Baba, xi, 35, 69, 75.
Lancashire Fusiliers, vii, 26, 27, 35, 96.
Lancashire Loyal North Regiment, 58.
Lancashire, South Regiment, 56.
Lemnos, 10, 76, 90.
Light Horse Regiment, 7th, 46.
Light Horse Regiment, 8th, 46.
London Field Company R.E., 129.

INDEX

Lone Pine Plateau, 22, 53, 75, 135, 138.
Lord Nelson, H.M.S., 7, 95.

M

Maclaurin's Hill, 29.
Maidos, ix, 15, 22, 31, 48, 134.
Makir Keni, 6.
Marmora, Sea of, 14, 47, 97, 103.
Mediterranean Sea, 1, 9, 13, 15, 38, 70, 91, 124.
Mendere River, 28.
Messina, 8.
Mitylene, 51.
Monash Gully, 41, 46, 75, 97.
Monro, General Sir C., xiv, xv, 71, 72, 73, 79, 118, 119, 120, 122, 123, 138.
Morto Bay, 7, 12, 40, 91, 93, 129.
Mudros, 10, 40, 60, 90, 91, 124.

N

Nagara, 14.
Narrows, xi, 4, 7, 8, 11, 12, 13, 18, 31, 37, 39, 52, 58, 90, 91, 92, 97, 98, 127, 131, 133.
Nek, The, x, 22, 52, 109.
Nibrunesi Point, xi, xii, 42, 54, 75.

O

Odessa, 8, 40.
Orkanie Mound, 7.
Otago, Mounted Rifles, 54, 99.
Outpost No. 2, x, 53.

P

Pasha Dagh, 16.
Pera Gelata, 6.
Peninsula, xiv, 7, 9, 12, 16, 18, 29, 39, 40, 49, 67, 72, 73, 76, 77, 79, 118, 120, 121, 122, 123, 128, 129, 133
Persian Gulf, 1, 3.
Pine Ridge, 22, 44.
Plateau, 400 feet, vii, x, 29, 52, 53, 94, 97.
Plugge's Plateau, 21.
Post No. 3, Turkish, xi, 55.

Q

Quadrilateral, ix, 46, 106, 108.
Queen Elizabeth, H.M.S., 7, 10, 12, 25.
Queen, H.M.S., 20, 97.
Quinn's Post, 29, 41, 46, 75, 97, 100, 119, 138.

R

Rhododendron Spur, xi, 56, 135.
River Clyde (collier), 25, 95, 129.
Royal Ark, H.M.S., 10.
Royal Dublin Fusiliers, 25, 26, 44, 95.
Royal Fusiliers, 26, 130.
Royal Munster Fusiliers, 25, 95.
Roumania, 3, 6, 89, 125.
Russia, 1, 4, 5, 6, 9, 40, 89.

S

Salt Lake, xi, 75.
Sari Bair, ix, x, xi, 2, 18, 20, 22, 48, 50, 52, 53, 54, 61, 62, 65, 69, 133, 135, 137.
Sari Tepe, 98.
" S " Beach, vi, 22, 23, 26, 27, 29, 30, 93, 95, 129.
Salonika, xiv, 9, 70, 71, 90.
Saros, Gulf, x, xiv, 12, 19, 51, 65, 67, 69.
Scimitar Hill, xii, 61, 63, 68.
Sedd-el-Bahr, 7, 10, 24.
Smyrna, 12, 31.
Serbia, 3, 6, 125.
South Wales Borderers, 2nd Bn., xi, 23, 55, 95, 97, 129.
Susak Kuyu, xiv, 68.
Suvla, xi, xiii, xv, xvi, 7, 35, 36, 48, 50, 51, 52, 53, 56, 58, 59, 62, 64, 65, 66, 67, 68, 69, 74, 75, 76, 134, 136, 138.

T

Talbot, H.M.S., 45.
Tasman Post, 44, 107.
Tekke Tepe, xii, xiii., 7, 26, 63, 64, 76, 96, 110, 130.
Tenedos, vi, 10, 15, 19, 92.
Triumph, H.M.S., 40, 104.
Turks, xiv, 2, 3, 4, 9, 17, 24, 26, 41, 42, 45, 50, 55, 57, 64, 65, 67, 68, 74, 78, 91, 92, 93, 94, 100, 120, 128, 134, 138.
Turkey, 1, 2, 3, 6, 9, 89.

U

U Boats, viii, 40.
Uveik, Dagh, 2.

INDEX

V

"V" Beach, vi, xv, 22, 23, 24, 25, 27, 29, 76, 77, 78, 93, 95, 96, 129.
von Sanders, General, 13, 15, 47, 52, 56, 62, 70, 76.

W

Walker's Ridge, 29, 97.
War Council, v, 3, 4, 6, 10, 14, 16, 32, 37, 39, 40, 48, 89, 90, 91, 99, 125, 131.
War Office, 67, 126.
"W" Beach, vi, xv, 22, 23, 24, 26, 27, 29, 76, 77, 78, 79, 93, 100, 129, 130.
Worcestershire Regiment, 26, 27.

X

"X" Beach, vi, 22, 23, 24, 27, 29, 93, 96, 97.
Xerxes, 17.

Y

"Y" Beach, vi, viii, 22, 23, 24, 93, 96, 98.
Yeni Shehr, 7, 28, 94.

Z

Zeebrugge, 89.
Zeitun Burner, 6.

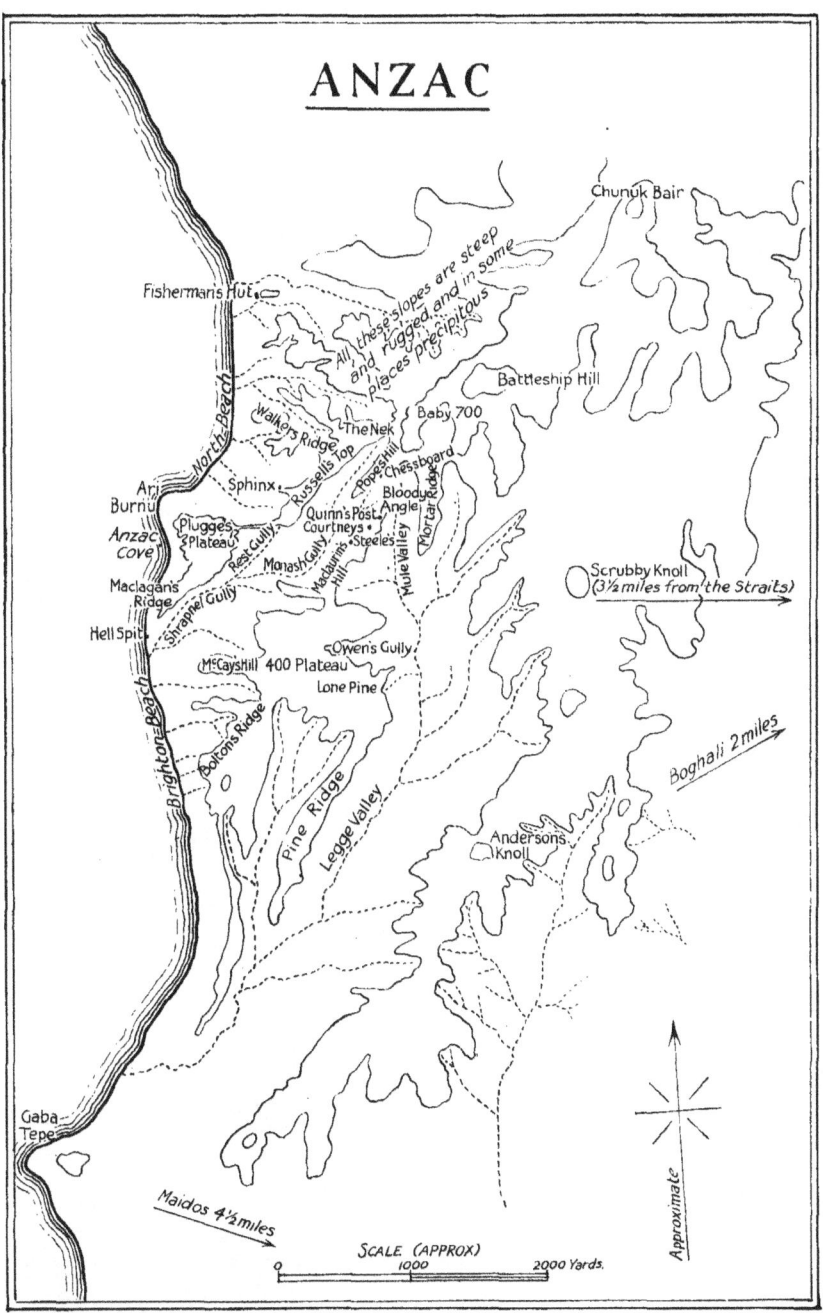

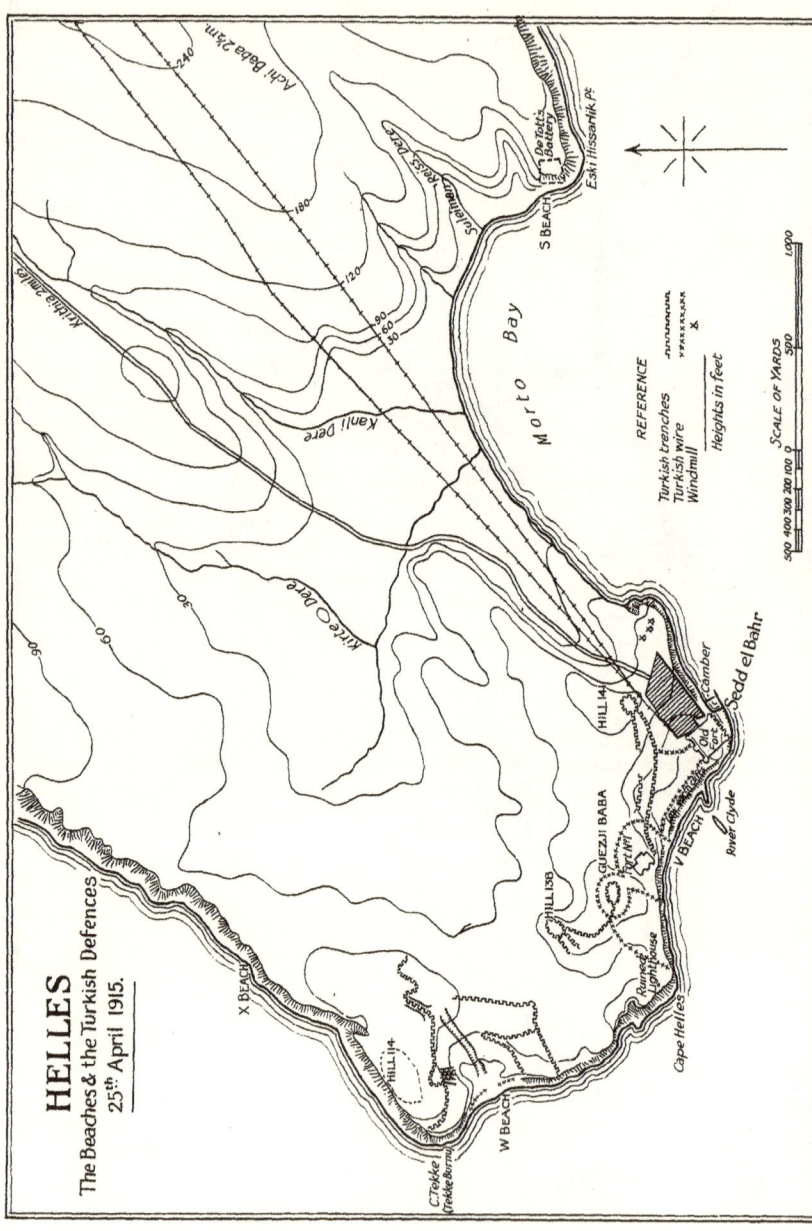

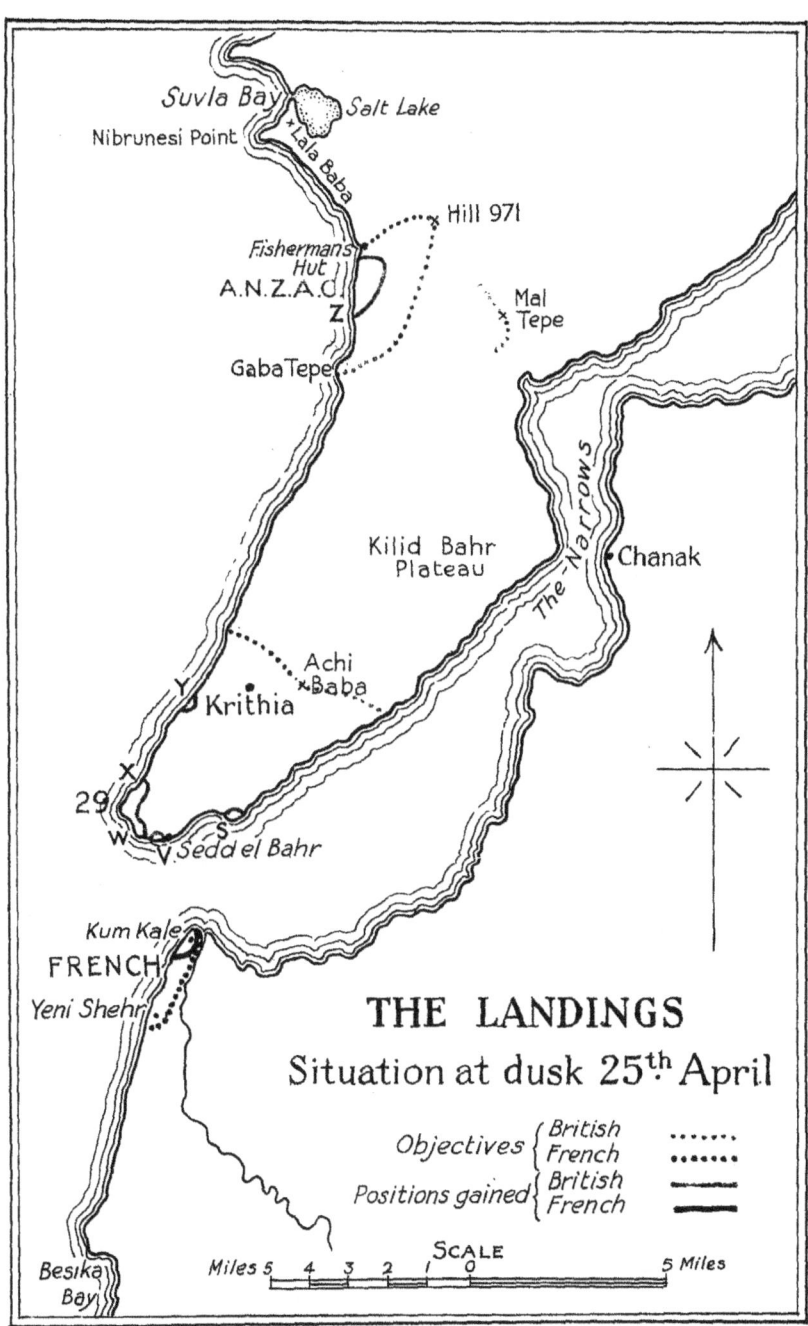

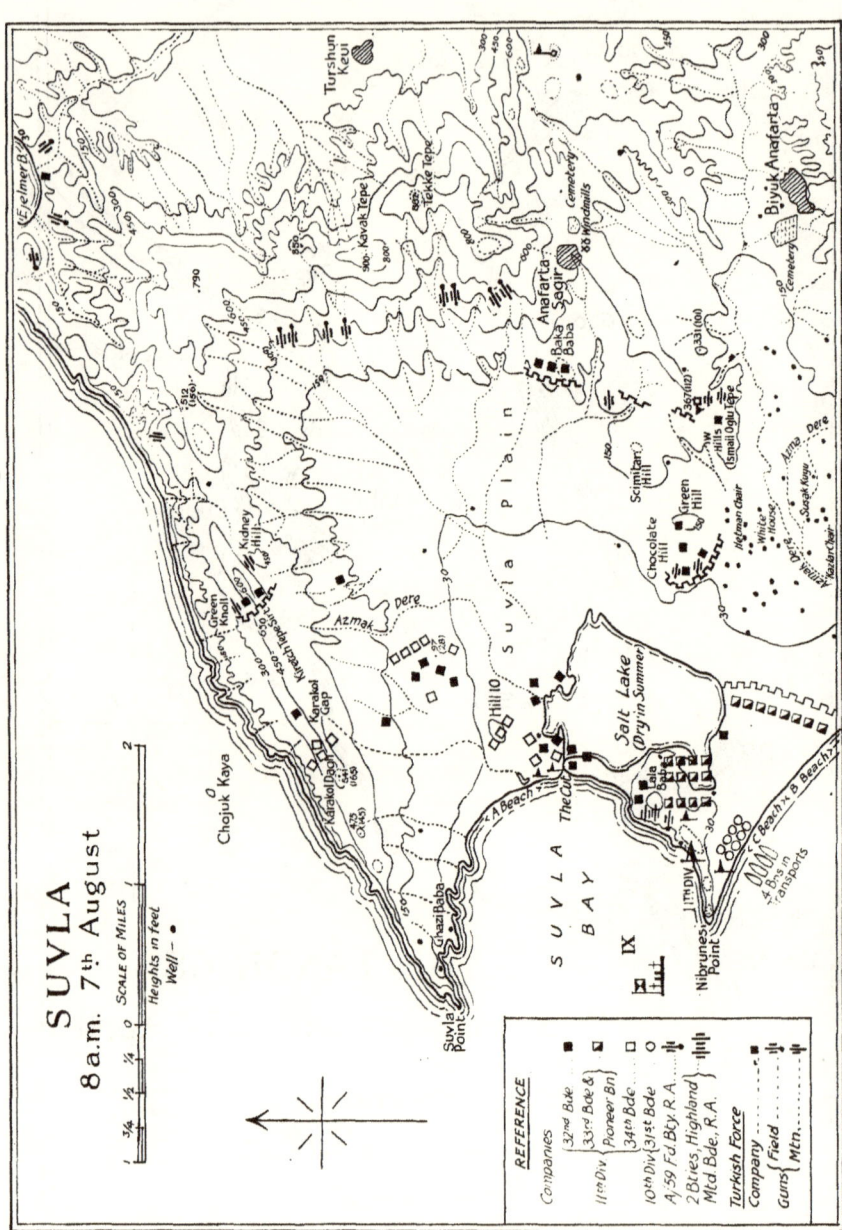

www.ingramcontent.com/pod-product-compliance
Lightning Source LLC
Chambersburg PA
CBHW031956080426
42735CB00007B/420